Symphony of Shadows

a Collection of Works by

The Black Rose Poet's Society

Cover and Artwork by Crow

© 2007 by Black Rose Poet's Society

All rights reserved. Each author of this collection retains exclusive rights to his or her poetry. No part of this book may be reproduced, stored in a retrieval system or transmitted in any form or by any means without the prior written permission of the author, except by a reviewer who may quote brief passages in a review to be printed in a newspaper, magazine or journal.

First Printing

ISBN
978-0-6151-5439-8

Printed in the United States of America

Published by Black Rose Publishing
Printed by Lulu.com

This book is available from Black Rose Publishing at
http://www.lulu.com/blackrosepublishing
and on most on line book stores

Dedication

To our patient and loving Families
and our loyal Friends

Forward

This book is a collection of works by members of the Black Rose Poet's Society. The one factor we all have in common is the desire to push the limits of poetry. There is no subject that we are reluctant to explore in our writing. Our purpose is to make people think and to deepen awareness of the human state of existence, the state of the world and beyond. Some of our poems are very dark, dealing with unpleasant subjects, others are beautifully descriptive, and others are deeply thought provoking. Our work is never for the faint of heart or for those who are looking for simple and superficial entertainment. We thank you for purchasing this collection of selected works from the Black Rose Poets and hope you enjoy the experience! The Black Rose Poet's Society can be experienced further at www.brpsonline.com.

Black Rose Poet's Society Members who contributed to this Anthology

Crow - Founder
Carol Digou - President
Susanne Psyris - Vice President
TinaMarie Buckler
Kerry Marzock
Susan Dano
Brian Damon
Anita Gates

Preface

Roses of Black

Misunderstood by some and criticized,
They write of all things light and dark.
Believing that light is the other side of a whole,
Knowing that true understanding is seeing the whole,
They explore the dark to find the light.
By knowing how dark we can be...
We humans who choose our paths freely,
They force us to face what we are.
By knowing the light that lies within us all,
They explore the dark to shine light on reality.
By knowing that true power is in knowing all,
They explore the depth and breadth of human existence.
Seeing through the eyes of others
To explore and share that perspective
Does not make that perspective who they are.
It is an art to reveal the truth.
It is a mission to reveal the whole of life.
It is a quest to enlighten by traveling through the dark.
For only by seeing the dark can the light be understood.
And only by seeing the dark can choices be appreciated.
If we are blind to the dark we float on the surface of life,
Never seeing the whole,
Never accepting the responsibility for the whole,
Never knowing the depth of our existence.
Never understanding the nature of the light.
All life is one and we are in all,
And all is in us,
And the key is in the understanding of it all.

© 2006 Carol Digou

Table of Contents

Crow 5
Gallows 6
Tea with a Demon 8
Between the Ticks and Tocks 10
Forever In the Darkness 12
The Haunting 14
The Bunny Suit Omen 16
Cradle of Sorrows 18
Ocean's Depth 19
World of Death 20
Pan's Gift 22
Woodland Meditations Within 24
A Perfect Picture 26

Susanne Psyris 27
The Mansion's Great Runes 28
Jerry! Jerry! Jerry! 30
Let the Sunshine 32
Asphalt Parks 34
Where Does Life Lead Us? 35
Ancient and Barbaric Tongues 36
Abortion's Aftermath 38
A Filthy Habit 40
A Single Indiscretion 41
And, So Comes the End 42
All the Damned! 43

TinaMarie 45
I am The Queen of Damnation 46
The Memory Remains 47
The Black Bride 48
Crucify Me 50
Morphing 51

    Black Roses' Black Sunday..52
    Lost in the Valley of Death..54
    O'er the Wretched Sea..55
    The Watchers II Web of Woe..56
    Jaded..57
    Do Not Stare...58
    Cold Cold Sea...59
    ~** With Liberty and Justice for All **~...............................60

Susan Dano.. 61
    After Life 62
    When Death Beckons..63
    Fetish..64
    Forsaken..66
    Slipping Away..67
    Stone Promise..68
    Sentinels in Shadow..69
    The End..70
    Quiet Refrain..71
    Tempest's Promise..72
    The Death Of Change...73
    Humanation..74
    Inconsequential Existence..75

Kerry Marzock... 79
    Fireflies and Bullets...80
    Rage...82
    Darkness Calls..84
    The Crow Man Cometh..86
    The Darkening..87
    Shadow Dancing...88
    Kiss of the Moon Beast...90
    Shadow of a Beast..92
    Night of the Sphinx..94
    The Fog..97

   The Gatekeeper..98
   Kiss of the Black Rose..100

Anita Gates... 103
   Angels...104
   Passing on in Soft Voice..105
   Skates Hung on the Wall...106
   Death's Lullaby..107
   The Boy..108
   Sylvia's World 109
   Gauche Masquerade..112
   Immaculate..114
   Coyote Ravin...116
   Fragments of Truths 118
   Nevermore 120
   Angelic Asylum 123

H. Brian Damon II... 125
   His Own Suicide 126
   Demon in the Priest..128
   Psychosis in a Padded Cell...130
   Lord of Dark Delusions...131
   If I am Screaming..132
   Shadow of the Harvester..134
   Auschwitz...137
   Dead Hollow Cemetery...141
   The Storm..144
   Of a Life Torn...147

Carol Digou... 149
   Metamorphosis..150
   Vigilante...151
   Venus (Fly-trap)...154
   Shadows of the Soul...156
   Introspect...157
   Hunger..158

The Moment Between..160
Message..161
Watchful Eyes..162
Song of the North..163
From Far Away 164
Epiphany..166

Crow

I am Co-founder of the BRPS Black Rose Poets Society. We are an exclusive group of writers who like to stretch the boundaries of writing to provoke thought and visceral emotions within people. We write poetry, short stories and novels. I am also a writer for the Inner Circle of Poets a charitable writing organization based out of Canada. I have a BS degree from William Paterson University. I am a 2nd degree Black Belt in GOJU RYU karate, 1st degree Black Belt in Iaido. I am also a certified Hypnotherapist, MCSE, CNA and NJ Special Police officer. After graduating college I returned to expressing myself through black and white ink drawings that were influenced by early European medieval wood prints. I took the concept and mixed it with a Dali sense of surrealism to create dark or horrific dream landscapes. From this was born Dark Gallery Art which I ran through the mid nineties. At that time I focused on my visual art work as well as running my martial arts school. With the advent of the Internet in the late nineties I decided it was time to get involved with technology, seeing many opportunities in the future. Presently I work in the technology field but once again find myself branching into art through the written word. My current projects include a horror novel as well as a book of poems. If you wish to contact me you can email me at CrowBRPS@aol.com.

Gallows

Solitude is the temple of the soul
A reflection bowl of gossamer
Dripping in spindles of ever twisting thought
Placid ringlets of lakes waves consumed by pebbles tossed by evil hands
Thoughts rolling on each current crashing on the shore of imagination
Wind swept stillness broken by soft crickets at dusk

I cup a pine cone feeling its sticky facets
Its monogrammed hem line like ginger cookies fresh baked
Stroking satin thoughts in my fingers
Looking at the corn cob forest dotted with kernels of colored leaves
Drifting punk weeds disturbed by the movement of bull frogs
Water skaters dancing on the purity that sifts to the top
Alone in reflection

Morsels of beauty sprinkle like confectionery sugar
Candy cane thoughts mixed with blood soaked clothes
The sum of all the injury and lack of love shown
Echoed moans of loons haunt this place of refined beauty
Of which I will never partake
But observe like a wounded bird unable to fly and feel the wind
Destined for only hate and a shallow grave

I strip away the dark clinging stain on mahogany boards
Sand the scratched wood and try to dress it in oak flavor
But the twisted boards are worn and broken
The structure slowly decaying under the watchful eye of weeds
Poison ivy of the soul climbing through the broken pottery of the mind
Unable to hold back the bitter tea that time makes me drink
My hands bound behind my back playing hide and seek with no one

I look in the mirror
Condemned as the latch to gallows sounds

A montage of faces smile
Shrieks, giggles, applause, revulsion
Their sacrament of death spoon fed them
I am their circus freak for today my neck stretching
But they should see the reflection in my eyes
Their cigarette stained fingers and sin clothed souls
Condemned to their lives of simplistic shallow joys

The screaming fades to silence
All that is left is the calling of the loons
The soft croaking of pond frogs beneath punk weeds
The scented birch wood fire and dusky night
As twilight finds me hanging in the wind

Tea with a Demon

Sitting in the coffee shop reading Voltaraine De Cleyre "I am"
The scent of Colombian beans brewing in pure water
Mahogany small desks, dusty books, a glass case filled with pastry
Dimmed lights and educated chatter
Echoing from the aged walls that have covered many a PhD

Spoons gracing cups with soft stirs and clanking sounds
Lovers exchanging hushed conversation in the shadowed corners
Old men enjoying chess on worn wooden boards

Out of the shadows comes a strange man unnoticed by others
Tall, bland, rather unremarkable wearing a rain coat
Funny how you remember the little things
The scents, the shimmer of sunlight, and the way a girl smiles at you

I introduce myself as Enlil de Palizon of course
You see when you have coffee with a demon never use your real name
It's the first rule of black magick and the rules are very important
He called himself Enzu but I am sure he has many names
He preferred a honey lemon tea with a bit of orange peel

We exchange contrite conversation for some time
All leading in circles as this is the second rule of black magick
Never ever lead a demon in straight talk
He is much older and wiser then you
Using truth and lies he will draw you away from the arrangement
Into something far worse and of course to his benefit

As I sip this delicate blend of rich dark coffee we get down to it
Immortality through writing in exchange for ….
Well that is not important but nothing as bland as my soul

He slips the price to me in a note written on the finest cotton parchment
Which I calmly pocket with indifference

He slowly rises bidding me a good day and a crooked smile
Taking care of the perfunctory displays of civil conversation he departs
Leaving his tea and me to relax in a pool of stagnant air

There you have my story my dear
Well the beginning anyway
If you desire more you must meet me here
Every Wednesday around 3 in the afternoon for the next 3 weeks

Rising from the old chair I wish her a good day
The young girl folds her Journal smiling beneath rimmed glasses
Her craft writing of course and her desire fame
To see her words read by others...by everyone touching many hearts

Sitting back she watches the steam rise from the cup of tea
A orange peel drowning in the honey lemon mixture
Funny how everything new feels so pure
Until you read the note in your pocket

Between the Ticks and Tocks

The pendulum swings drifting into the stir of silence
Hushed whispers freeze upon cold winds
Chess pieces lay upon a board of marble unmoved
Steam frozen on lips of lovers' smiles
Everything standing still yet I am in motion

Between the ticking irons of the watch is a secret world
Between one and two is an infinity of numbers
Between black and white a never ending amount of shades
Between light and dark a spectrum that goes on forever

I move among the brush strokes of artists
Leonardo, Van Gogh, Picasso, Dali
Oil colors bent into images of the soul
Transcending the ticks and tocks of time
Each new spirit gazing upon the colors with a new thought
Seeing a new line, a curve, a color, a motion

Lovers kiss before the paintings over and over
Each life playing out as did the other just with new actors
Moving to the chorus of inner thoughts found within the silence
That place between the ticks and tocks
Where eyes meet and know they have seen each before

You rise before the new sun
The light bending in infinite shades never the same twice
Revealing a new beauty that yesterday did not hold
It crests the white blossom tree flowing in summer's wind
Casting shadows on the new emerald grass

Something familiar stirs within the silence
You feel home again and at peace
Away from the clatter of busy streets and inane talk
Thoughts wandering between the ticks and tocks
Searching for the missing pieces of a puzzle not yet found
But desiring to know the answer

Forever In the Darkness

The scent of bleach burns my nose
A sterile darkness fills this place
The room black as pitch except for a line of light
Beneath the door
I hear them moving in the blind spots
Creeping things, stinging things, those that hurt me at night

A little dead girl in white comes to me with red eyes
Her coffin dress stained with fluids of some kind
Her breath of rotted teeth makes me vomit
She hands me a dull razor covered in dried blood
As I hear the insects coming closer
Ever closer across the floor

I feel the sting of their pumping abdomens
The scratching of their legs
Centipedes, hornets, scorpions, spiders of all sizes
Injecting me with venom
Feeding on my live flesh as I scream
Struggling locked to this hospital bed
Help Me God
But he never comes does he?

A dwarf with no legs slithers toward me
His bloody stumps leaving a trail
Hatred in his eyes as he screams
Released from hell to find pleasure in my pain
Ripping at me as his eyes role back white
Pulling my hair
Feverishly trying to choke me
The little girl laughs and dances in her shiny black shoes

As I take the razor screaming as my flesh swells and burns
It will not end ever
Help Me God
To the silence
I feel the steel cutting deeper into my veins
Releasing my anguish unto the floor in iron scented red
Pumping my sickness away from me

The nurses come in screaming for some doctor
Paging Dr. Sanity clean up on isle 12
I smile hoping it's over
Help Me GOD
Nothing
Get them off of me I yell beating the air
The rush of a needle pulsing into me
Sedating me
As I fade into the static white of a lone neon bulb
Forever in the darkness

The Haunting

The scent of fresh stain covered the scratch marks
Nails still embedded in the soft timber
Screams echoing in the lonely New Hampshire night
Above the sheep pens and dirt floor barn
The deep fall cold moaning through rattled windows

There she would sit
Stricken with some strange disorder
Some malady of the mind convulsing in swears
Talking like a man
Soiling her tan sleeping gown as she screamed
It's on me, touching me down there

They built a cage that sat alone in a dark room
A flight of raw iron metal stairs
Circling up there
To it

The thing that raped her with invisible form
Her body pushed down by weight unseen
Her hands pinned to the floor screaming
As the family tried to sleep in uncomfortable tears

They said it was some form of mental sickness
Breaking down on that old forsaken hill
The long winters of lonely and desolate reality
The constant gray of the harsh New England sky

But many believe it was a demon
The possession of her from the burial ground beneath the house
The dead that could be felt watching you as you bathe
Hidden eyes that make you turn
To feel the breathe upon your neck
But nothing is there

Many nights I slept with one eye open
Hearing the groaning of floor boards
The shaking of shutters
The rusted hinges of doors

On occasion I swore I heard whispers of screams
Echoes from that room in the middle of the night
Crying out for the lord who never came
Its sound making me shake
Trying to discern the howling wind
From pleas to God
Sounds of haunting memory buried in that house

The Bunny Suit Omen

Maybe it was the way he stirred his coffee
The scent of cheap after shave and bad use of the English language
The way the bell clanged when anyone opened the coffee shop door
I don't know
My mania was fixed upon conception and that is all I know

I have rancid hatred for those walking on two legs
Mindless sheep void of thought
Unable to breach the matrix of social confinement
The mental barriers of proper behavior, morality, sin
Defined by perverse men with gray beards

I stood there pouring the milk
Watching it swirl into the deep black myopic liquid
The scent of fresh baked muffins pervaded this place
I stirred three times to the right the fourth to the left
My eyes glued to the spittle in the corner of his mouth
As he chuckled hitting on a sixteen year old waitress

In the corner a gray man size rabbit sat reading the paper
It looked more like a bunny suit to me
No one took notice other than an occasional glance
So I did the same

He was wearing a pocket watch called dooms day
I could hear it ticking to the beat of a hooker's head motion
Then the ever present mumble of background conversation hit me
I could feel the sweat pouring from my head
My heart racing as the pain hit my chest
The bunny looked over smiling

I fell from the chair
The ceiling fan moving in slow motion
The man with the crusted spittle giving me mouth to mouth
So I could savor the flavor of humiliation
Reviving me to my death
It was then in my paralyzed horror
I knew
Society had consumed me

Cradle of Sorrows

Black silk crests the ornate carriage
It sits alone in a park of shadowed gray tones
A baby rattle dripping with condensation
The chilled wind moans through the lonely landscape
Twisted trees lay draped in November's frost
The ominous clouds releasing pellets of ice
Slowly unto a barren pathway
The wheels frozen in a puddle of mother's milk

A small cry echoes in desperation off of the cement bridge
Cobble stones fall to the ground
Graffiti licks the somber walls with shallow thoughts
Painting images of desecration
Images of filth and violence

The gas lights flicker on
As the crying rings out even louder
Puffs of frosted breath steadily rising
The carriage sits abandoned on a secluded path
Away from helping hands
Away from eyes of pity and hope
The wind moans louder as the cold air moves in
The park casts shadows of night's dark embrace
The cries growing fainter in the solitude

It is the cry of humanity within the vast universe
Abandoned by the powers of it all
Left to the desolate realization that there is no salvation
Struggling to live within the vast cold of space
The darkness
Of the universe and the human soul
So each of us struggles to survive our own journey
In the cradle of sorrows

Ocean's Depth

Reflections prism aqua sunshine as gulls float above
I'm standing on the shore as waves roll beneath my feet
The cool sand pulling me deeper into the vast mystery before me
The sun rising from darkened horizon as beauty sings its song
A single beam of gold striking me in morning's illumination
Fallen to the shores of ocean's depth
Crafted through deep dark eyes

Is there anything more beautiful than the face before me?
White caps burn with violet fire off golden skin
Delicate curves carved in nature's perfection
Waters warm lips kissing me deeply
Transfixed at how perfection moves
I wonder as I hear the waves roar

Such a being of power yet so gentle
Delicate and soft melting the hardest rock
Smoothing out the edges
Brushing beach wood the color of satin alabaster sheets
Its power like electricity through me
Making me numb as the sun rises higher
I can see more of her
Her inner depth
The hypnotic melody of her voice like sirens' call
Crashing against the rugged coast of my soul

At any time the waves could crush me like a delicate bottle
Shatter me into a million pieces of broken glass
Instead the oceans hands hold mine
Leading me to the cool waters
A place of relaxation and warmth beneath the burning sun
Honored to even touch the shores of her mind
Muted by such beauty I stand silent
Just observing the wonder of you

World of Death

The raven sat plucking the eyes from the dead
Its beak suckling the fallen fruit of man
A necropolis of barren flesh once housing a soul
Each one a being endowed with a higher spirit
Slaughtered by the siege of ideas and banners
Caught in the climax of good and evil
Slain

The chain of never ending death sings on
A melody of hysteria that reaches beyond technology
It seems the bastions of civilization at their zenith
Can not hold back the ideology of destruction
There are honorable causes when one must fight
Against the evil insanity of other men's souls
The brutality of their own selfish desires
But the result is the same
Be it war or on a city street

Death is no respecter of persons
Good or Evil we all bleed out our life force
His black mouth only knows the consumption of flesh
Destroying bone and muscle
Destroying the minds and spirits of all that observe
His black wings descending in murder

We will never grow beyond the veil of evil
Selfishness, power, sexual brutalization
These are the mother's milk of a small boy growing now
With plans to spread his ideology of destruction
To feed upon his inner desires of hate and slaughter

Death
Destruction
Pain
Misery
Suffering

Rain is not the moisture of fertile clouds
It is the tears of the damned crying out
Dear God stop the killing
Pouring unto the ignorant below
Each generation born into a world of death
Each generation trying to live on a planet of blue
Shadowed by a universe of ultimate darkness
In which some consume their souls

Pan's Gift

Minstrels dance before the fires of Hephaestus
Orange, gold, crimson flames forge the flutes of pan
Silver and Gold dripping of wine leaves and carved acorns
Slowly worked by ancient hands to awaken nature with their song
As Vulcan's hammer echoes through lush green woods
Drawing fawns to its melodic beat

Sitting back against a large rock sipping Bacchus's wine
Cool, crisp, crushed from the richest purple grapes
Taken from lush green vines planted by Dionysus himself
I put the bottle on the moist dark rich earth soaking in nature
Feeling its power flow through me and all that is

A Saffron sky ablaze in flames before the twilight hours
Purple crested mountains roll majestically into foggy valleys
Shimmering waters drip from twisted trees
Running from the carved cliffs falls of crystal
Enchanted pools and lakes of placid beauty

A stream plays its ancient song at my side
Whispering passion's sweet kiss from Venus's lips
Running through reeds, over rocks and fallen branches
Twisting among the water lilies and bathing frogs
As the forest and water melt together under Aphrodite's winds
Moaning in the shadows

Pan sits waiting for his newest flute
Reading the poem I pen for him from ancient quill
His eyes a soft deep green shimmer as he scans the parchment
His thick curling black hair adorned in a crown
Golden oak leaves and acorns twisted upon vines of ivy

From his finger he takes a ring of silver
Carved with the face of the green man and Pan's very flutes
Ancient as though worn a thousand years and one day
The four elements infused in its living metal
Melted and bound in earth, air, water and fire

He hands it to me as Diana's Moon burns from shadowed branches
The night has taken this place of oak, maple, birch and elm
I hear Artemis stir awakened by the flutes of the coming dawn
Pan rises with a playful smile disappearing into the mist

The crickets play a soft symphony
The cool winds blow through scented pines
As the ring I take forever mine placing it on my finger
Flying upon the winds of song from a gold and silver flute just born
To slumber's nest I rise to play among the stars from ancient days
In this world of visions pure I see Pan's gift forever more

Earth, Air, Fire Water
In me they all reside and I within them
A child born of nature's womb delivered by cosmic hands
As is the silver ring I wear
Forged within the myth of time a child of the true divine

Woodland Meditations Within

I sit in silence beneath the birch, oak and maple canopy
Woodland branches twisting into Diana sky
Illuminated by the soft golden glow of scented candles
They sit upon an ancient gnarled oak stump
Cascading cinnamon wax dripping onto dried dead leaves
Forming faces of future's destiny upon the rich dark earth
Melting into copper images of fortunes soon to be
Health brimming from the flesh of the asp and cedar
Passion dripping from thorns upon a twisted vine of rose wood
Breathe in deeply the cool fresh air
Let it caress your mind and purify the spirit

Sitting in Pan's predawn amethyst light I enter that which is within
Listening to Bacchus stir to life drinking deep the intoxication of nature
Wet concord grapes glistening purple born in this place of Magic
A cool woodland pale mist flows through thickets and brush
It surrounds all in love's white protective embrace
Grounding my thoughts

I look upon the waters of this black bowl made of copper
Gazing forever into the placid onyx depths
In the murk of mystery's shadows an image appears
A red rose dripping golden dew from each petal
In its center an opal of brilliant white
It speaks to me in sleep's soft whisper touching the corners of my mind
Bleeding crimson words from thoughts spoken on full lips
In the solitude of self I hear that which talks from within

Incantations cast upon the sweet pine scented winds of the gnarled woods
Lucid images flow deeply from the black bowl like memories
Times of joy and moments of pain

Languishing in crystal dreams of sentient pleasure
Splashes of passion's prism cast in fire
Projecting lust and love upon a canvas of warm flesh
Visions of childhood dreams

I sit in solitude
Recharging myself for the coming black storms ahead
Languishing within this moment of peace
Until the waves of humanity's sorrows roll over me again
For now I smile within the woods of self

A Perfect Picture

Pale blue mixing with aqua emotions
Foaming waves rolling into charcoal craggy rocks
Slivers of golden light cascading on the morning surf
A prism of a thousand thoughts
Swept onto shadowed beaches

Gulls circle weathered boats
Drifting into early morning's fog
Searching the vast ocean of reality for their treasure
If only for the moment

On a piece of bleached drift wood a spider spins a thread
One single silken dream that catches the salted winds
Rising delicately it drifts along the sandy dunes
Where ever it comes to land it will build its life

I take my brush from the canvas
Unable to capture even an ounce of the beauty I see
I turn to share that which is before me
But only the cool wind caresses my face

The beach is empty except for the show of nature
The flowing changing textures, shadows, colors
Each one rolling into the other
Like the waves before me

Will this beautiful memory live on after death?
Or will it fade away forever into the coming night?
A perfect picture lost to my mortality
Lost to the solitude of my thoughts

Susanne Psyris

I am a native New Englander. Although, I have lived in different states within the U.S., my home has always been with my family in Massachusetts. My love for my family has been one of the most powerful cornerstones in my development as a person and a writer.

I write from the heart and soul, expressing my deepest emotions and fantasies upon page after page, leaving pieces of myself for others to relate to and learn from. Though much of my writing dwells in the recesses of the dark and forlorn, I have a strong propensity to write along the spiritual vein.

As a member and then the Vice President of the Black Rose Poet's Society (BRPS), I have grown both personally and professionally. My first book of poetry, "The Infernal Abyss," was a dream realized only after my introduction to the BRPS. Each and every one of my fellow Roses has positively influenced my writing ability and I am very proud of my association with them.

The Mansion's Great Runes

Who lives within this Black Rose Mansion?
Sordid souls, erupting passion?
Beyond the crumbling walls and moat,
Whose voices through those halls do float?

Though from afar, its eerie presence
Instills a fear that becomes its essence.
For those who jaunt within its range,
Life's energy does become too strange.

The Mansion, postured high on a hill
An entity that emits its own will
Upon its keepers who do surmise
The walls of the Mansion do have eyes.

Eyes that pierce like knives to the soul
Ever watching and in control.
The keepers blinded by the unwritten trust
Trod cautiously away from swords that thrust.

Each knows their place to bid their deeds
None ever denies the Mansion its bleeds.
The carcasses and rotted remain
Gifts for the One who rules the domain.

Words and pictures etched into moss-covered wood
Surrendering to evil, but not chastising good,
Are found throughout this magnificent place
But of the owner, not one claims its face.

For the Mansion feeds on the the very souls
Of its keepers presented in various molds.
So very distinct and so different, each one
But a powerful flow that continues its run.

In the chill on the bridge that crosses the moat
Stands a frightful man beneath his long coat.
The sword that he carries to render his prey
In the night, 'neath his coat, is hidden away.

He waits patiently from dusk until dawn
Never uncertain of the One who comes on
To watch from the tower for any who stray
And once they are his, they can't get away.

But the man is unwelcome by the keepers all
He is but a dark creature to hasten the fall
Of lost souls and misfits left behind
And treasures for the One who makes no sign.

Those who feed the Mansion its fare
Are always present and ever there
Writing their muse, and intricate tales
Of blood dripping ceilings filling up pails.

Voluptuous beauties in black silk and lace
Are rampant and wild, and at times a disgrace.
They pick with their hands the flesh from your bones
And fear not the One whose wrath they condone.

For others are left outside the grand gate
Never to realize what would be their fate.
If found within the Mansion's great runes
The keepers all would manifest their doom.

Who lives within this Black Rose Mansion?
Sordid souls, erupting passion?
Beyond the crumbling walls and moat,
Whose voices through those halls do float?

Jerry! Jerry! Jerry!

Cockroaches crawling
across sweaty flesh.
Greasy,
fatty lard,
thick and hot,
clings to the air.

Babies wallow in kid shit
squished in dirty diapers.
Mothers engrossed in Jerry
just don't care.

TV bellows torrid tales
on daytime soaps;
Neighbors fucking neighbors
on the sly.

Nothing making any sense,
chaos reality;
soiled linen on makeshift beds,
no one questions why.

Junkies shoot shit
deep into collapsed veins.
No one gives a fuck
that children go insane.

Bleeding Drops of Angel's Tears

Visions of fire and brimstone ~
The great burning lake
Filled with the charred bones
Of sinners cast into the pit,
Sink deeper into the mind's eye
With every word written
In the Book of the Damned.

Crimson-colored flesh,
Drenched in the sweat of pain
Sizzling to the touch,
Falls off skeletal remains,
Oozing like pus
From an open sore
That never heals.

His life rejuvenated
By the blood of new babies.
All beginnings ending at birth;
Proverbial bad seed
Shatters the silence
Of sad mournings as
Mothers weep softly.

Thunder crashing!
Lightning bolts strike...
Black clouds hang low
Bleeding drops of angel's tears
Upon lonely hearts
Seeking refuge from
He who rises from the Abyss.

Let the Sunshine...

My stomach ached and gurgled
I lay there on the hard floor
In the long corridor of the hospital
Among many others that day
Waiting to see a doctor.

My eyes blurred and my mind numb,
Unable to decipher the images
Trolling through my muddy brain,
Stung with tears that exploded
Onto my pallid cheeks.

It had only been a couple of hits
Of Orange Sunshine swallowed down
With bourbon straight from the bottle
On a stomach that hadn't seen food
In more than three days.

There had been many nights
That it seemed I would end up here
Just like this, a smear on the floor
Shaking out the withdrawal
Half conscious of my surroundings.

Later, lying in the hospital bed
Spitting chalk into the bedpan
Black powder ring around my mouth
Vomit drying on my chin
I would begin to recover.

The irrational juxtaposition of objects
Began to redefine themselves
And the growling sounds
That escaped my lips began
To form coherent words and sentences.

"I didn't die, again"
I would tell myself,
As sweet sleep embraced me
And the IV dripped quietly
Through too thin an arm.

Asphalt Parks

Sun climbs to its acme ~
pours heated golden rays
onto black asphalt parks
where children play.

In the city ~
where the forests
are made of steel meters
and street signs,
they play hide-and-seek
in abandoned buildings
painted with graffiti;
windows shot out.

Mother yells ~
out of dingy open window
where clothes lines
display tattered and worn garments
passed down more than once
to the youngest child.

"Frankie" she hollers
down the long, trash littered alley,
"Come home to eat."

Dinner is waiting ~
for a dead child
laying in the dark
surrounded by water rats
needle still hanging out of his arm.

Where Does Life Lead Us?

Death follows me through the days of my life and
lingers at every turn waiting for me to fall
in to its tormenting grip ripping my soul to
the sounds of echoing screams that fill the
center of my mind and make insanity a thing
of salvation from the mundane ways of
my sorrowful existence deprived of
soul and a means of escape.

I listen to the thundering voices in my head that
fight among each other and thrash about as if
to take control of my entire being but I
live and I breath and I am alive at this moment
but do not take for granted imminent death
the days of forging ahead with strength is a
battle that I have become too weak to fight
is this the end of all that I have known am I
lost to the evil ways of demons and the evil one?

Floating as angels over my being
above my dead body I cling to life
my soul soars to the sky in brilliant light
lifeless entity lays beneath angels wings
corpse of mortal being now passed.

I open my eyes wide to a wondrous sight
see the gates of heaven open wide to enter
clearly St. Peter is calling for me
the Book of Names, I am written within
price of love and goodness prevails
that I may enter Heaven and find God's
love to carry me throughout eternity
does the burden of following the Word of God
cost more than the price of the Devil's tithe.

Ancient and Barbaric Tongues

They spoke in ancient
and barbaric tongues,
a language known among
whores and thieves
whose misdeeds
would be inscribed
In His book
by which they would be judged
come the end of time.

God was angered
by the lack of dedication
and meditation
devoted to Him
by the masses of atheists
and, worse...
those who called themselves
devout Christians
but never knew His word.

He sent plagues,
created disasters,
slipped into their very souls
and waited for their love
but found only ill-will
filled their hearts
none able to impart
beyond their own want
and desire
the spark to light the fire.

The end of time came
the multitudes gathered
begging to enter
the Gates of Heaven
but, found Satan
was now the Keeper of the Gate
and for them, for all eternity
they would burn
in hell's fires.

Abortion's Aftermath

I weep for those who'll never see
Christmas gifts beneath a tree,
filled with candy canes and popcorn hanging free;
or, hear the tale of the "Wise Men Three".

And, too, for those who'll never hear
the jingling of bells of Santa's reindeer
hauling gifts of toys, games and "Baby Sweet Tears"
that the children will cherish and hold dear through the years.

The caroling choirs
circling barrel-filled fires
will spread Christmas cheer
to all living here.

And, then, again'
as the tears blur my vision,
I'll realize you'd be ten,
but for my selfish decision.

The bunnies, the candy, the egg-filled baskets,
are symbolic to me of the vacuum-type caskets
that literally ripped you apart;
my poor, sweet embryo.

Your tiny, frail limbs,
your soft, slow pumping heart,
abruptly destroyed by medical know-how;
discounted, abolished, terminated,
from God and from life with no known peak.

Forgive me, my seedling, my Springtime conception.
But, myself, a mere child; I believed this deception:
That a seed in the womb is not life in true form;
That the egg was not living;
That no child had been borne;
That the pain you'd inspire would outweigh all the pleasure;
That the demands you'd require, would extend beyond measure.
And, now barren and broken and poor in my health, soul and mind,
and sharing the joy of other's children - none mine;
there's a token memento mori - a lifetime haunt:
That risking and daring for that uncommitted jaunt,
bore not children to love, but pain, shame and want.

A Filthy Habit

I reach out for it, it invites me
Like a heroin addict, I always return for more
Never believing that I am slowly dying
Never to see what tomorrow has in store.

The mucus is like black-strap molasses
My lungs tighten with each breath I take
Excruciating pain shoots through my chest
Feels as an impaling with a large stake.

I spit out the slimy nicotine-based phlegm
Wipe the corners of my cracked mouth
Suddenly I am heaving into the porcelain
Breath is rasping and terribly foul.

I inhale deeply, the smoke is like salt to an open wound
The pain is strong, but the need is much stronger
I watch the gray ash as it softly falls into my lap
And, exhale unable to hold it within me any longer.

I convince myself that this is the last one
That I can stop without going insane
But, one right after another I light them up
My fingers decorated with the nicotine's stain.

I reach out for it, it invites me
Like a heroin addict, I always return for more
Never believing that I am slowly dying
Never to see what tomorrow has in store.

A Single Indiscretion

Like a cool breeze
in the heat of summer
she dances upon his sweating brow
and casually drips into his being.

Unseeing,
blinded by salty perspiration
he cannot wipe her memory
or the anticipation of her touch
from his mind.

Shining brightly
the sun hovers over his body
as he lays upon a craggy rock
by the swiftly flowing stream
and he screams for a love lost!

What cost, this heavy price
for a single indiscretion:
his depression.

And, So Comes the End

Wind's gale, howling in the night
Fright of every cowering child
Mild words of love condensed
Incensed by what is vile.

Fear grips and carries through
True that monsters 'neath beds lie
Try to hide from all that's evil
Still in the night, comes the sigh.

The devil's called his own to war
For reasons that are very clear
Near is the end of the world we know
Slow is the death for those so dear.

Hear the hooves that trample now
How they come to all who'll see
Free your soul, God listens so
Know in your heart, God says, "You are Me."

All the Damned!

Claw-like hands
reaching up from the pit
scratching,
digging,
into my flesh
pulling me
downward
into the belly of Hell
where my hopes
and dreams
become my fears
and nightmares.

Struggle as I may,
I cannot free myself
from His torturous grip
as I feel my soul slip
into the blackness below
to wallow in the abyss
with all the damned
who preceded me here.

There are loud cries
"Help me Lord!"
screamed and echoing
in my mind
as I try to find
God.

TinaMarie

My love for reading drew me into poetry. Poe and Dante' influence my writing a lot. I am naturally a dark poet, if that's the proper term for how I pen my pieces. I usually don't refer to my writing as poems but rather pieces, as they mirror me in some way. I write with heavy metaphors and graphic descriptives. If you can read between the lines, I am in each of my poems. I am by no means a professional writer, I am a novice and always appreciate when people like what I write. I want to thank my husband and three beautiful daughters, Amber, Camille and Mallory, for always supporting me.

~Pushed down so far
deeply buried within
hidden from others
my tormented sin
Hold it all in,
let no one else know
what you have witnessed
bottle that crazy shit up
Don't Dare ever cry
suppressed feelings denied
cannot infringe upon
my already, Tormented Mind.
In all that I am,
with every fiber of my being
no matter how hard I try
to deny what I'm seeing
distorted images flash
faces contort, screaming
I cannot unleash from
these torturous demons,
so you will find
my hollow soul
In purgatory, Swinging~

My writing can be graphic so I warn you in advance and I thank you as well.
*** I want my Fellow Roses to know that without them I wouldnt have the courage to put my words into print. You all are a bunch of brilliant writers and I am humbled to be a part of this group****
Peace My Friend, ~TinaMarie
*Minions Mosh the Caustic Pitt, Headbangin to Demonic Riffs**

I am The Queen of Damnation

I dwell in the darkest caverns,
Lifeless cold brown eyes
pale white skin and blood-stained lips
I am Lord Satan's Concubine.

Hidden underneath the twisted folds
of my flowing Purple laced gown,
I wield an inverted crucifix to impale,
your wretched soul to the ground.

I condemn thee to vengeances death
drag you down the road of perdition,
LeVey disembowels your bloated corpse,
the Dark Masters' divine revelation.

My throne lies, at the devil's right hand,
Spewed forth out of lust and temptation,
Bore from the loins, of Hells' Succubus,
I AM ~The Queen of Damnation.~

The Memory Remains

On a jagged path I'm lead
gagged, upon the stench
spewed forth, from unholy ground
to eternal darkness; bound.

Beyond the realm of death
betrayal, pricks my flesh
damnation's fury unearthed,
The Tainted Goddess; cursed.

Flung deep, in a pit of hell
my blackened soul now dwells,
trapped, in this rusty cage
thrashing, from fits of rage.

No hope of being free,
stagnant, within misery
in acid tears it rains
clanks, the ball and chain.

The Sullen Goddess cries
praying only, now to die
suffocate, in torturous pain,
tho' Your Memory Remains.

The Black Bride

It is time....
An antique dress of Midnight Black,
Red roses entwined with thorns,
blood trickles down her wrist, dripping
Crimson droplets on the floor.

Tempted to indulge thy forbidden fruit
Lured by seduction in her eyes.
He has watched her forever, and
Tonight she becomes his Bride.

Heretics dance among the alters fire
Sinful souls shade the night
To consummate their darkened vow,
The Kechi Priest begins the rites*

"Do You Black Bride take thee thy Lord? Give
unto him, your body and your soul?"
"I do." She replies

"Do You Lord Craven,
take thee bride In torture and in Sin?
Deny her nothing, and do with her thy will?
"Yes, I will all this night and many many more.
I will delight in her body and dwell in her tainted soul." Craven replies.

The Priest raises his chalice.

"A toast to thee Dark Lord and Tainted Goddess
May you rule this wicked realm,
for all eternal darkness!"

A music box whines morbidly out of tune
Their shadowy figures waltz around the room
Pale white skin, she's hauntingly pristine
Cold to the touch she barely breathes

Descending the spiral staircase,
her lace train sweeps behind,
Casting light from the depths below
As they open to welcome their Bride
Quite delicate in her features
Something he's coveted all his life,
Whispers honey in her ear
and sings, a cacophonous lullaby.

Raspberry red champagne flows
The Lord twirls his tainted bride
Chaos reigns the Kingdom
Ravens circle, the tumultuous sky
Formed from Hells decay,
Lord and Lady Craven
Ghostly Soul Mates,
Created by Satan...

Crucify Me

Sullen's the Queen
dark sins to atone
wondering lost
destined to roam
Fear it defames
her spirit and soul
lost in the shadows
no place to call home
Destined to lose
untouched and unseen
swallowed by darkness
consumed in a dream
Can't dwell upon
unhallowed ground
destined to suffer
Twisted and bound
No one to save her
withered by lies
nobody cares
destined to die
Forged by destruction
breeds a bloody melee
Light the cross on fire
and Crucify Me...

Morphing

Teetering, a thin fine line
on the brink of my demise
smell the searing of my soul
in a fiery Inferno I will burn~

Lightening flashes, thunder claps
heart beats wildly within my wrath
drift on bitter tears of hate
tormented river I hath create

Morphing within a demented mind
twisted memories I cannot hide
dreading total chaotic doom
they come in darkness to forge my tomb~

Floating on a tortured sea
foreboding evil claws at me
invades my every waking dream
rapes my psyche in misery~~

Black Roses' Black Sunday

The B.R.P.S

~It is within these shadows
the thirteen disciples gather
pay homage to The Queen,
and their Black-Feathered Master.

Enticed by a melody
lures the melancholy violin,
the Symphony of Darkness
Black Sunday shall now begin.

"Heed me minions on this day,
for it is the holiest within,
Our Grand Society."

Crow raises a toast of crimson hue,
"Go well dark minions, I bid you adieu.
Time is drawing near, my evil fiends
We will rule this realm
with the demon seed!"

Lord Craven was spawned from sacrilege
it rots his nefarious soul,
Created by hellfire and the Devil himself
Some 400 years before.

Loyal minions mosh furiously
drums pounding the rhythm of death,
"Caw Master Caw!" they start to chant.
"We are the soldiers of

the Black Rose Mansion,
Where Anarchy rules
and Chaos our mantra.
Chant our black bible
as we march through the castle
Loyal till Death
We follow Our Master!"

Violently contorted bodies
hung on flesh hooks
swing from chains,
the walls dripping
thickly coated,
Screaming red
with tortured pain.

Descend deep within the Mansion
Black disciples engulf the masses.

~The Sacraments of Hell shall begin on this day,
The Black Roses' Black Sunday~

Lost in the Valley of Death

Last night I walked through the valley of death
devil as my guide, holds the book of the dead.
he tallies destruction with an evil grin
for the Wars of man have started again

Sky lit by fire, blood of innocents rain
he revels in screams of their tortured pain,
lurking in shadows the reaper awaits
'til the Master calls him, to deliver their fate

I cover my ears, I can take no more
he battles my spirit to gain control,
a limp marionette tied to evils hand
he twists and contorts me
to finish his plan.

On the brink of demise, God save me please!
as nefarious demons pull me to my knees.
The devil laughs, "Where is your God?
He has forsaken you, just like before.
I am the ruler of, this realm of death,
Now surrender your wretched soul,
And your earthly flesh."

As I lie, gasping for one last breath,
he covers my face with the hand of death
through the fiery gates of hell
I am viciously flung,
Blood-lust angels hail Satan
my purgatory has begun...

O'er the Wretched Sea

~Swinging o'er the wretched sea
tears of torment scream for thee
locked inside this rusty cage
in a darkened corner, fade away~

Sullen are her tearful pleas
hang on a chain of misery
heart is all but now forsaken
love harshly stolen, vainly taken

Trapped and woeful in this cage
so long since the light of day
has trickled through the rusty bars
or softened cries of bitter sorrow

Spirit crushed beyond recognition
wicked dreams within my vision
rippin' at the throbbing vein
floods my soul with acid rain

~Swinging o'er the wretched sea
tears of torment scream for thee
locked inside this rusty cage
where my flesh turns cold, and
~decays~~~~

The Watchers II Web of Woe

Writhing in my web of woe
the faceless one won't let me go
contorted within a bed of lies
rabidly he feeds off my bitter cries

His forked tongue darts and whips
"Marked you are," he begun to hiss
"come on now, just give in
no use fighting you cannot win.
I've been summoned by Satan
to collect your soul,
You've been branded
now pay the toll."

Impaled by a hook he drug me down
clawing and screaming but not a sound
passed over my dry swollen tongue
the death bell now, tolls for one

Fog rises from the bowels of hell
cackling demons chant and wail
Deumus rips my soul to shreds
hollowed my heart left me for dead

Harpies peck what's left of my brain
Sullen tears, all that remain
twisted and broken I feel no more
entombed within my web of woe...

Jaded

Within tears of sorrow
collected through the years
heart bitter and hardened
torpid in my fears
love has become jaded
fallen into rage
spirit sullen and faded
trapped in a rusty cage
dangle above a hole
to much to forget
fighting for my soul
memories rot my flesh
eyes swollen shut
demons in darkness revel
psyche splintered and cut
I've become a hostage to the devil~~

Do Not Stare

She thrashes wildly, against the padded walls
Black-Rimmed eyes lifeless, no soul
speed-metal banging in her head,
lithium takes control..

She's floating now, so surreal
sweat stings her swollen eyes,
a smile erupts from her blood-caked lips,
she mouths something, out loud.

"Save me" she pleads, stretching out her hand
Lost in a realm of illusion,
Longing to touch the man of her dreams
alas, he's just a delusion..

Reality is, the dimly lit asylum
sinking, into the hollow ground
her bleeding, beating heart devoured
by a three-headed feral hound.

Cold Cold Sea

Trapped in the dark recesses
within a corner of my mind
Claw marks down the walls
from trying to get back out.
Your obvious lies are slowly
sucking away my breath
tearing apart my sullen soul
'til it's flapping in my chest
Left flailing in the cold, cold Sea
Your sinful betrayal is drowning me
Let me go, set me free
Your choking the pitiful
life right out of me...

~** With Liberty and Justice for All **~

*to MY fellow dog-face soldiers*3rd ID

If no one had Personal Courage
or convictions for our beliefs
If warriors didn't sacrifice
Tell me where you'd be?

To Honor our sworn Duty
Against all our enemies
With Loyality and Respect
The American Soldiers Creed

If Bravery didn't exist
or Integrity did not stand
If there was no Self-Less Service
Would this be the promised land?

So we hold our heads up High
Stand tall and drive on
Wear our Uniforms with Pride
LIBERTY AND JUSTICE FOR ALL

Susan Dano

I was born on the Saint Lawrence River, in the midst of the Thousand Islands in Upstate New York. The country up there is a rich and fertile landscape for my imagination, even when life got in the way. I moved from there at the age of 23 to Fort Richardson, Alaska, leaving my Father and Grandmother sadly, resting in Peace in the same cemetery I played in as a child.

Leaving there after 3 years I moved to Las Vegas Nevada, my mother, Nora and various relatives still reside in the North Country and so does the inspiration for most of my efforts at writing today, Ms. Campany, my 12th grade English Teacher. I will never forget the words that she had posted on the wall that greeted us everyday. "Carpe Diem", Seize the Day. Those words inspired me, as did this most glorious example of what a teacher really is. The other shining light in my life, my Princess Olivia, is responsible for inadvertently driving me to become better at writing, and driving me insane in the process. For these things I love her with everything in my heart.

I don't have any more education than a high school diploma, and what life has taught me, although I am aspiring to take Criminal Psychology, and I haven't won a Pulitzer Prize... yet. I have achieved writing excellence and the only place to go from here is higher.

Also, inherently, I wish to add that without the support and understanding of a mad cap, motley group of Black Roses, this would never be possible.

I am macabre, fanciful, and I am dark, but I am me and that is all that I can be. This is what I believe everyone should aspire to be... Themselves.

After Life

Raindrops softly falling,
trying to wash away,
words cut in stone.
Unforgotten memories,
Lost in time.

Grim, empty gray, sky,
Viciously , driving down tears.
Silent as the grave, opening my arms,
receiving the lashing,
the cold, purifying my soul,
Throwing back my head I laugh.

Eyes closed, chest heaving,
unholy screams,
echoing against the slate walls.
My knees, falling...
sinking into the breach.

Slowly opening my eyes,
the moon, shrouded in clouds,
fog blankets the ground.
Enfolding me, where I lay.

I can still see her name;
it has not changed,
still dated two weeks ago.
And I weep like a child.

When Death Beckons

Did you ever feel like death;
Was opening your window,
Waiting with baited breath;
As you walked into the moonlight?

Did you stand there?
Silently screaming in pain,
Raging at The Machine,
Wanting to end it all?

Seductive nothingness,
Beckons with a kiss,
A crimson tipped finger,
Curls in your direction...

While a legless boot,
Smashes into your spine,
Presses into your windpipe,
And grinds unmercifully...

I am coming...
On whispered winds,
Over trickling waters,
Riding charcoal wings of the Raven...

Never mind... I am already here.

Fetish

Dusken rose petals,
Scattered, across crimson silks,
Jasmine wafts in, from open windows,
Mingled with scents of hot leather,
Anticipation burns within me.

Blood coppery and sweet—
Lingers upon my swollen lips,
Fingertips, caress milky thighs,
Blistering wax forging a trail,
Across tight planes of flesh.

Arms leaden with burdening chains,
Staring, hypnotized at candle flames,
The kiss of his whip crashes down,
My body, seizing in satisfied agony.
His smile is silent in the darkness,
Coarse hair shadows his jaw line,
Whispering across my battered skin.

Shuddering, ecstasy so close...
Bubbling up, ready to explode,
He drags cords across bruising flesh,
I cry out, whimpering a pleading moan,
Humiliation bearing down, as I cry out.

He relents and drives into me,
Thrusting over and over, grunting, heaving
Exploding within me, with a scream.
Bittersweet satisfaction at last...
Intensity, the likes I had never known...

He falls into me, holding me close,
I am lulled by his beating heart,
Sweat slickened bodies, converging,
Soft murmurs of cherished loved...
I whisper his name as I close my eyes.

Forsaken

Tonight, death beckons...
How I ache to answer,
Reaching out longingly,
For silent release.

Allowing myself to be raped,
Daily, in unexpected way...
It claws at me for more,
As this mind drifts away.

Lovingly, I accepted it,
Blindly, bestowing my trust,
Relinquished a bleeding heart,
Only to swallow, bitter ashes.

If I could cry,
Would it ease the pain?
Letting the weakness inside;
Spill out like putrid rot.

Disgusting Whore,
Ridiculous Charlatan,
Manic Obsessive...

Silence is my only recourse,
For no one can salvage me,
I cannot unchain myself,
Death Beckons tonight...

On gossamer wings of ebony,
The only entity answering.
One more whispered oath,
As I give myself to Oblivion.
Once again... a Child Forsaken.

Slipping Away

Every thought was clear... like drops of rain,
Muscles, vigorous and robust,
Skin, sun kissed firm and taught,
Unblemished by time and toxins,

Glossy silken strands of hair,
Lifting and flirting with errant breezes,
Eyes glittering with anticipation and hunger,
Now, lost forever in hazy memories,

Adamant dreams of more came to naught,
As my heart was dragged deeper into misery
Only to rise again then beaten deeper into hell,
Somewhere... someone is laughing,

Laughing at my shattered reflection,
Know this... I will not remain shattered eternally,
I will stand, clenching my fist, and I will howl,
Vengeance will resonate from my very soul,

And you will feel it all—
Slipping away...

Stone Promise

One stone at a time... a fortress was erected,
The jagged marble- each piece a lesson in agony,
Thick walls of impenetrable might stand silent.
Drawbridges, eternally closed, No admittance.

Dense undergrowth of thorns have grown to the tallest spires,
Come forth... I dare you... fall upon these living daggers and die.
Bleed as I have bled, scream as I have screamed...
Then rot away as all the rest have done.

Some hacked at the thorns, tearing away piece of me,
Looking for an entry, an easy victory, a trophy, a battle scar...
Others, forewent the thorns, and carefully scaled the walls,
Digging their instruments of destruction into my soul,
Only to be pitched from the highest point, crushed to the earth,

No more shall they pass, I am forsaken, haunted,
I will see them fall away into oblivion,
Phantoms all, in the ethereal mists of memory,
As my gut wrenching sobs echo in eternal darkness,
Henceforth I will bear the burden of my sorrow alone.

Sentinels in Shadow

The Mother falls to peaceful slumber,
As she trades autumn tresses for snow white strands,
Everything makes ready to embrace her descent,
Calmly aware she will awaken in gowns of hunter green,
Dancing within the songs of sunrises and twilight mists,

There is no sorrow, only resigned acceptance of her absence,
Coupled with merriment, and celebration of her return,
For within her much deserved slumber she dreams of you,
For now, the Great Stag steps out of the silent shadows in all his glory,
Surveying her children, acknowledging their birthright,

Under Father's watchful eyes, the great provider, guardian,
Standing silent as the cedars watching over her prone form,
Caressing her peaceful face with the heat of summer promise,
Striking with the force of ten thousand fists, at those that dare harm,
He lends a deep, patient whisper, into your ear–

Know that you are never abandoned in this life child...
Your Mother envelops you within her loving arms,
Father wills away your mournful tears,
Our counsel will always be there for the taking dear one,
Ask but in word or deed, we will guide thee through the veil.

Each takes a hand, pulling you to your aching feet,
Cry as you cry, laugh as you laugh, love as you love...
Walking the Path with you, letting you fall, teaching you to rise,
Only a soft spoken plea away, no matter how hard you push away,

So waste not such a short existence in mourning,
Fighting against the lessons that you must learn,
Reach out and grasp every possibility to laugh,
Touch sadness to appreciate the glory of joy,
Remembering always, you are never alone.

The End

This abysmal day must end...

Let the curtain fall, allow night to blacken the sky,
Willing silence to choke off even the whispering wind,
While traitorous tears slip down my face.
'Tis far easier to be lonesome in the darkness
Where none see the quiver of your shoulders
Or note the hopelessness in your eyes.

O' to have strong capable arms embrace me!
Sure rapture exists only in fleeting dreams,
So I dream... each night bitter sweetly,
With the suns ascent, I regretfully awaken,
Monotonously, I exist, feeling no purpose.

And so, I will dress in my finest couture,
Bathe my skin in my finest potions,
Turn the minored music low,
Lay my cheek against a satin pillow,
Watching, as my ebbing vitality,
Falls softly... in a stream upon the wooden floor...

Finally... the pain is subsiding...
At last... this abysmal day has ended.

Quiet Refrain

Stinging raindrops,
Fall against lucent glass.
Sliding down panes, blurring before me,
Effusive tears fall inside,
Weary for my release.

Lost in surging rivers of agony,
I crash against rocks of uncertainty,
Struggling for footholds in repose,
Drowning in Should Have Beens.

Momentary bliss, so precious.
Fleeing just as swiftly,
A taste of happiness,
Viciously ripped away.

Sweet harmony has gone,
Tender melody, dying,
Invoking wisps of memories,
Envious of my youthful ignorance...

All I wish is quiet refrain.

Tempest's Promise

I will shake you...
Terrify you...
Watch without empathy as you fall,
Give you respite and rip it away...
Just to see you weep.

Confuse you...
Tempt you,
With promises of reprieve,
Then drive you to your knees.

I am supremacy. I am might...
I am... I am... Rage!
A lesson learned in the harshest way,
I am pain, suffering and agony...
The embodiment of trials and misery,

But I am your savior...
I wash you clean, purify you...
Ripping your iniquity away,
To reveal a new beginning,
I am your humility...
I serve, to make you strong.

Make your way within me...
I will be the demise of your adversary,
Standing within my chaotic arms...
I will entwine you in a lover's embrace,
Decimation... I am the Tempest.

The Death Of Change

Creeping slowly into The Great Nothing,
All hope lost, pleasure turning to dust on your lips.
Now, you are prepared...

Before being choke slammed back to Reality.
Where suffering is a broken floor, terror, blood drenched walls.
And a ceiling is caving in on top of you.

Where do jagged rocks end and soft sand begin?
When eager waves, can joyfully caress endless shorelines?
The first stabs of realization drives deep into your flesh,

Losing so much time cringing away from psychotic illusions,
Find yourself kneeling within the maelstrom that offers no pain.
Incomprehensible... strength bears you up upon obsidian wings.

Becoming aware, you are the agony...
Knowing you form the storm, not drowning within it...
Temperate trade winds replace biting gales,

Knowledge, empowering you to rise and stand,
No more the slave, but mistress of emanate domain,
Finally, you have mastered the Death of Change.

Humanation

Unspoken infiltration of instinctive appendages converge,
Razing a swath of devastation in their wakes,
Accurate ignorance in travel size convenience,
Oh how we fought in bitter arrogance ...
Only to be restrained once more, within pillars of silence...

Scorching them within searing flames of agony,
Burying them deep in hushed earthen barrows,
Drowning them in rampant flood waters,
Ripping them apart with Herculean winds,

Yet, a million more ascend to take their place,
Never ending waves of mindless destruction,
Ebbing and flowing like poison in the bloodstream,
Sapping the strength of Earth Mother ,viciously,
The anguish has become unbearable, we feel her quivering...

Standing at the four corners awaiting our time again...
We bear her soundless pain with her,
Weeping with obsidian tears as we await the instance...
She can bear no more.

The Zealots renamed us for terror that we instilled,
Plague... Pestilence...Famine and War...
Hoping to instill their lambs with fear for their device...
We will be realized one day for what we were known for all along...
The End of Man... Death... No Salvation

Inconsequential Existence
A Collaboration of Thoughts
from Tempest (Susan Dano) and Nomad (Brian Damon)

Crimson sunset glistening upon prosperous fields,
Bathing strands of wild grasses in blood tinted waves,
Unease, settles upon the narrow minded populace,
Sending shudders of apprehension through the masses,
Prelude to evisceration, forewarnings unheeded,
Ancient fears rising up in debauched souls,
Prayers begin their ascent to an indifferent Empyrean,
The Blades of the Reaper begin their descent.

Within the populace of immoral desires and emotions
Degradation of the soul begins as the apprehension builds,
Watching the growth of their enemy just outside the city gates
As they mass in the blood stained fields of the previous slaughter.
Human in nature yet animalistic in actions, they appear supernatural.
Each one carries a scythe, curved to a wicked point, and gleaming.
A faint breeze carries an arcane sound to the city walls.
Chanting in Enochian, this army of death's design, gathers in formation.
The smell of decay, rotten and rancid flesh assaults the city first,
Then as one they disappear from sight, yet the chanting remains,

Convergence of the unseen, within deafening silence,
A pregnant pause preludes winds of swift revolution.
Beautiful demise... observed in aporetic awe,
Until humbled by your own private demons...
Permeating you with piercing shrieks and shrill reminders,
Kneeling in its midst, wallowing in decadent indulgences,
Swelling your gluttonous throat until bursting forth,
Enveloping your covetous chattels in bitter bile...

Feeling it build within your soul's constraints,
Slowly but deliberately invading your mind, body and soul,
Blades of the Reaper continue to fall, destroying your inner self.
Husked shells of what once was, wander aimlessly through the streets
While the Reapers demons instruct them with heinous thoughts
Stars shining down with sadness, weeping light, so as never to forget
The madness and degradation concluded upon now unhallowed ground.
Blood of innocence and madness, mixed in pools of stagnant devastation
Befouling all it touches, tainting even the once purest water source.
Vile unrelenting evil begins its spread through the land with the seepage
into the water.

Darkness descends obliterating the infinitesimal shards of light,
Filling each fragile moment of quivering silence with dread,
Pouring into jagged minutes of misery, enriching each crevasse
Eradicating honeyed virtues, replacing it with untold perversion,
Harvesting pain with open mouth grins, with each hitching sigh,
Glutting nonchalantly, with every torment wracked heartbeat,
Where hope stood in a pillar of salt, shining like virgin crystal,
Only a tainted ocean of lamented tears remain in its place,
Eternal Damnation... the only palpable deliverance,
Absolute salvation...a prelude to unmitigated evisceration...

With each and every drink from the bloodstained chalice,
The villainy spreads throughout the land infesting and afflicting,
Ritualistic sacrifice begins with hopes of stopping the progressing tide of
evil,
Further fallen the blades of the Reaper, annihilates all in its path,
Growling like Hell hounds, the horde of demons descend again,
Angelic children once, now gutted in the arms of an aberrant father,
Society shatters as trust is corrupted; and fear is a god,
The lost souls are scurrying to their corners in the dark...
Down on blood encrusted knees, begging their idols, even now...
For a promise of peace... a reprieve from a never ending horror...

Once again, willful pride goeth before the darkest descent,
Empires lain to waste by the infantile hands of their creator,
Chill silence, the only monument to this prevailing civilization,
Where naught exists, and no one recollects,
Gentle tides fade away as russet wild grasses encroach,
Ashes to ashes... Dust to Dust, until the morning dawns,
Thousands of meaningless lives, and their worthless creations,
Nothing more than silent whispers on ancient winds...
Vague uncertainties lying in darkened shadows,
The tremble of sorrow enfolding their innocent hearts,
That the oblivious populace remembers naught.

Ghosts of times past roaming through corridors of once majestic city
Openly weep at the loss of memory of the horrors endured
When the now rusty and pitted blades of the Reaper ruled supreme.
Rebuilding of demonic destruction, slowly wiped the remnants away
Until it was only fabled, then legend, and now completely forgotten.
But the ghosts they remember and are seeing the signs that point
Straight into the waiting arms that desire forging another blade,
One that shall never lose its power, gleaming finish, and stay razor sharp,
That will subtly call the howling hordes of demons back into the city's heart
And the Reaper shall once again reign terror and anarchy upon them all.

Kerry Marzock

Some children run crying and screaming at the sight of something awful, frightening, or monstrous. I embraced it, enjoyed the titillating fear and allowed the darkness to smother me where I felt safe. It was blessed escape as were all my books and scary movies. I ventured to far off planets and adventures on other worlds written specifically for me by the great science fiction and horror writers. The characters were me and the beasts were creatures that I fought and defeated. Then I magically became those beasts, or at least the majestic wolf. Frankenstein was too big, ugly, and rusty. Forget being encased in miles of tape as was the Mommy, plus it was death personified. Speaking of the living dead, the Vampire was fear and romance combined, but sorry, still cold and dead. Alas, the wolf and alteration to another form, to feel the power of the beast and to race underneath a moon full of delightful promise, a living, breathing creature that could alter shape. As a child, change was important for me, and so I became enamored at the thought of escaping my body and being somebody, or something, completely different. Anything but me! So when I first saw Lon Chaney standing by a lonely tree in the fog after being told by the gypsy woman he was cursed to become a beast under the full moon, and then changed from man to wolf, I was hooked.

Writing is an escape and I've gone through stages where I wrote a lot when I was younger and then something called life stepped in the way so I hardly penned a word for too many years. Maybe it takes a life threatening situation to make you realize that life is too short and you need to grab hold of the things you like and want before it's too late. So I began to write again, letting the emotions pour out in my poetry, mostly in tears, but changes of the heart as well. Being a voracious reader my teachers were the great authors I read, hoping their brilliance and creativity would someday wear off on me.

Darkness can be frightening, but darkness is also my friend. As a result, I've written my first horror novel, "Raven's Rage", a rousing werewolf tale set in Philadelphia. It can be obtained on www.amazon.com. I am currently working on the second Raven novel, as well as my first fantasy tale. I am also collaborating with a wonderful musician on my first CD and am very excited about that as well. In addition, my book of poetry "A Sea of Emotion" can be obtained on www.publishamerica.com. When my mystic wolf howls, I am free. Change is hard, but worth the fight. I let my emotions fly with the intensity that feelings need to possess in order to convey their true meaning. Otherwise, the emotions are flat and dull, unhappy and empty. I hope my poetry and fiction writing is enjoyed as I have enjoyed all the wonderful writers who have given me so many hours of escape and wonder. Presently I live in Philadelphia with my husband Richard and wonder dog Rain.

Fireflies and Bullets

Neon splashed atop the cracked pavement
of a bleak, crime-ridden city street,
reflecting garishly off sightless,
soil smudged, haunting black windows.
Gutters littered with broken liquor bottles,
lipstick stained cigarette butts, and
three day old syringes, devoid of false dreams
and empty hopes. Sad refuse of fractured
lives searching for salvation from final drops
of bitter honey, or at the end of soulless,
disease ridden needles of temporary pleasure.

Somewhere in the distance a loud bang
shattered the quiet, unearthly stillness.

Inside the corner park one solitary, still unbroken
street lamp glared angrily down upon
a rusty swing set, one lonely, empty seat swaying
slightly from the push of a hot, stifling breeze.
Harsh light from the one glowering lamp
lightly bathed several half-comatose bodies
lying upon whatever brown grass remained,
or sprawled atop paint-chipped benches,
dreamless lives at sea somewhere between
abstract dissolution and bitter reality.

Somewhere nearby several sharp pops
echoed madly down a dark alleyway.

On the edges of this surreal darkness,
like a splintered string of Christmas lights
blinking on and off in rapid succession,
were the flickering lanterns of fireflies,
un-phased by surrounding poverty and pain,
drugs and soiled dreams that stained
the skin of those who had given up.
On and off, the tiny lights glittered gaily
within the darkness, a small armada of smiling
Tinker Bells, peek and twinkle, faultless sparkle.

Down an alley a loud explosion shakes the
blood stained bricks as a bullet seeks the flesh.

Behind the blank and sightless windows
are eyes that witness nothing, even if they do.
Beneath sheets of newspaper atop park benches
the numb and comatose do not move, fearful
there is one more bullet seeking death. Upon
the brownish grass lies a fresh body, coppery
scent of blood spreading in a stagnant pool.
Above this black pond the fireflies flicker on
and off, on and off, like lights from a deadly
carnival of the absurd, one more fatal statistic.

Far off the pleading wail of a siren,
another gunshot heard,
deadly bullets passing through
a flickering ocean of fireflies.

Rage

gentle, yellow sunlight bleeding
onto soft horizon...blistering like a river
of molten wax melting from a candle once
aglow with love, now...painfully snuffed out
within never-ending seconds by quivering fingertips,
spiteful words of hate stinging and clinging
to soft lips that once were kissed,
now achingly bruised...from darkened thoughts of...

RAGE

a heart once meant for love
awash in torrid sunset now turned blood-red
Soft sand from a glittering white beach charred black
from years of corrosion and erosion, sinking
into love's haunting song, tragically gone wrong.
Oh, please let these fingertips reach for keys
upon this lonely keyboard rather than the sharp,
steely blades of animosity and hatred.

RAGE seething

as the fury of hell's hateful winds crash and burn
upon the edges of darkness, while evil eyes of Satan
grin, reaching out with claws dripping with blood.

Whose blood?

These hands and thoughts painted crimson as sins
of the transgressor scream loudly toward the heavens
for just one last caress of happiness.
Sunlight revealed...desperately reaching out
to touch the plush softness before
it slams to darkness.

ENRAGED

Darkness Calls

The fetid, nefarious breath of death lingers ~ ~
fingers draped heavily across my shoulders
like a monstrous shroud,
a malingering cloud
of tarnished dreams that tries to
suffocate my terrified screams.

Sighing, someone's crying out
as absolute darkness whispers in my ears, grating ~ ~
scraping painfully down my spine.
Shifting sands of endless time spilt
from a fractured, shattered hourglass.

It's so damn cold in here!
Anguished thoughts quiver painfully
within this plaintiff plea of supplication,
swirling river of salvation raging ~ ~
waging a battle of lost hearts, reaching out
to touch a spark in this feral darkness.

Far off a pin prick of light from within
forever constant midnight, appearing ~ ~
nearing where I float amidst mind-numbing anxiety.
Screams of long forgotten dreams assail my senses
as I see a deranged face emerge from darkness.
It grimaces and attempts to touch me.

I cringe as bony talons scrape against my cheek.
Startled eyes fly open, this frantic heart
now beating insanely ~ seeking ~ peering ~ ~
at my own reflection disappearing in total blackness.
My urgent hand falls frantically across the sheets to

lie upon bittersweet rejection,
as unholy darkness calls out to me again.

The Crow Man Cometh

Darkness reigns
upon these fractured dreams
~~like chocolate~~
bitter sweet upon the tongue.

It slowly sweeps
before these eyes and seems
to block beatific visions sung
in melodies now stained
under dark and lonely skies.

Let death
be not the answer wished as
sorrow steals your
final breath.

~~Listen~~

to the blackness creep
upon these broken hearts
as wings of darkness
call us home
where nightmares
never end in sorrow
shared alone.

Sky expands and cries aloud to empty
tears now shed upon tomorrow.
For day is done and night
shall never cease to be,
black wings of death
sweep over me.
Dark and evil crow man coming
soon for me.

The Darkening

Inside darkened thoughts I pace these halls,
grimmest mask of dire death upon me.
Hear the hiss of evil cry out in tortured minds,
with crimson blade of steel our downfall.

It appears but once upon the bluish moon,
this devilish breath of blackened ash.
Rank stench of blood pervades the air,
my steps the tragic echo of silent doom.

Future hopes are lost ~ this darkened soul as well ~
no point of prayer ~ Hell ~ no one left to heed me.
Listen to the chorus of inner demons moan a song of death,
haunted howls of midnight where only darkness dwells.

House of rooms all painted black, all but save the candled light,
seems to fit this evil heart that breathes within me now.
Blood droplets drip from honed tip of steel
as the beds upstairs reveal such ghastly sights.

Sane thoughts now lost ~ a hiss from Satan's sleep.
A tap of tiny fingers now rap upon my door.
Red blade clutched tight, this darkening enshrouds me,
as childish voices echo ~

"Trick or treat ~ trick or treat."

Shadow Dancing

Can you feel it?

Slithering around your ankles
like thin bands of stale cigar smoke,
swirling in a grotesque embrace,
dancing a dirty tango
against quivering thighs.
Indecent shadows playing a childish
game of tag with fading thoughts
of yesterday, mocking fractured dreams
of lost, unrecognized tomorrows.

Do you see it?

Through a haunting, whispering darkness,
two chilling eyes stare in a lascivious glare,
their angry sordid color
that of dried blood splashed across
a barren, lonely sidewalk.
The vacant, midnight glow of
an estranged street lamp casting
a final, eerie spotlight splayed over top
misbegotten hopes.

Could it be my blood?
Perhaps it's yours.

The sharp glint of something silver
floating on the edge of a pulsing
blue light from a searching
police car, shadows dancing

gaily to a song of forbidden destiny.
Long, jagged fingernails claw at the flimsy fabric
of sanity, eliciting a startled scream of terror.

Did you just scream?
Perhaps it was me.

The night is nothing more
than broken promises
and shattered dreams. A lonely time
when fears become your only
life line, sodden with hungry tears
grasping for those last threads
of happiness. A howl of forgiveness
breaks the silent stillness …..

Eyes fly open,
startled to awakening.
Darkness floats on slithering
shadows, dancing on the window
to a flickering light of blue.

Kiss of the Moon Beast

For me......while I lay silently draped quivering
within velvet darkness, the ending was simply
the beginning. To feel death steal my breath away
on a moon-splashed, neon night was both
frightening and exhilarating.

Clearly I knew what awaited me
as I gazed hungrily into those eyes
of golden, smoldering passion for I was now
enraptured ~ ~ ~ captivated ~ ~ ~ enslaved ~ ~ ~
I remembered the fateful night so well, to forever be scratched
within my mind, branded for all eternity upon my heart.

Your feral lips brushing mine and whispering,
*"If I asked you for your life,
would you present it to me now?"*
"You have but just to ask," I whispered back.
I felt your tongue snake eerily against my neck
and shivered icily into the vast unknown.

*"If I held your neck within my urgent mouth,
would you scream in unholy terror?"*
"To scream is but to fear, to moan
is but simply my deepest surrender," I groaned.
Tensing, I felt the sharpness of your fangs
scratch the soft surface of my skin.

*"If I beseeched you to accept the beast,
the wolf who rules the night, would you do so now?"*
With frantic heart pounding, I stared wantonly into
a savage face of wild, terrifying, supremely powerful beauty.

"I am nothing but yours to mold and shape, for with sweet death
arrives the pain of rebirth. Let your hungry kiss
be the mark of beast I so yearn to now embrace."

Fearful, yet anxious, I shut my eyes
to welcome the blessed pain to caress me.
Exhaling my final breath of lost humanity,
darkness spread forever until I felt the pounding
of a savage heart and listened to the haunting lament
of a wolfish howl brush the skin of a glorious, silvered moon.
I opened my newly feral, golden eyes and sniffed the air.
**"If I asked for your eternal love,
would you merge your beast with mine?"**
Glaring into a ferocious night, I howled with sweet desire,
"You have molded me within your own image.
Oh my sweet paramour, this love for you will last into forever."
The moon smiled down with giddy delight
upon the back of beasts that now prowled the night.

Shadow of a Beast

As my fingertips angrily strike the keys I see
the longer hands of a shadow moving eerily
in a slightly different direction from my intention.
Extending my right hand, frightening fingertips
of shadow slither like a serpent over the keyboard,
caressing the dark brown, wooden surface of the desk.

Startled, I note that they are elongated and sharp,
like claws of a creature ~ the fanged and furry beast
I write about ~ the beast that forever haunts my
fractured dreams which create my stories.
Glancing through red, sleep-depraved eyes
I read about the innocence that once more dies.

Closing my lids to the burn of tortured insomnia
I pray that I will stay asleep, no more words of death.
***"Open your eyes and write about me, about us,
about the power we possess together, the strength
of unity between humanity and beast. OPEN NOW!"***
The voice was low, guttural, seeming to come from me.

The keys clicked and clattered, driven by fingertips
turned magically into vicious talons, blood on the
'd', and the 'e', and the 'a' ~ can't take this insanity.
My anguished head moves as does the ominous shadow.
Who's shadow? Not mine ~ CAN'T BE ~ muzzle long
and narrow ~ it turns, grins ~ drool dribbling on pages.

Heart pounding, I look towards the blurry screen,
harsh, white light glaring, black letters breathing,
like they have a life of their own, fetid breath of madness

so intense it cripples me with fear, fear of what it means.
Darkness moves in to replace the sinister shadow,
last waking moment seeing auburn fur upon my hands.

~ ~ ~ ~ ~ ~ ~ ~

Upon awakening, the morning newspaper lay before me.
Startled, horrified, amazed, the headline screams to me.
"YOUNG COUPLE SLAIN IN FAIRMOUNT PARK"
"Witnesses swear they saw a large, wolf-like creature."
Tripping and stumbling towards the desk ~ my haven ~
I wait with bitter disquietude, fearful of what I'll see.
The stark manuscript appeared and with breaking heart
I read of murder, death and mayhem in Fairmount Park.
Tearfully I saw one long hair still clinging to my hand.

Night of the Sphinx

Bewitching time is but the sweet breath of night,
feral whispers sifting from a silvering moon
awaiting the explosion of a vibrant sunrise.
She calls forth to defile the beguiled,
sweet demonic daughter of the Chimera ~ ~
intoxicating Mistress of your fate.

Moving to the swirl of biting sands
with the sway of haunting palm fronds,
she dances ~ she twirls ~ she spins to evil madness ~
pounding heart of a lion surging to come alive,
bathed in moonlight before pre-dawn's awakening,
nighttime breezes singing loudly for beasts to thrive.

Listen closely to the crackling winds ~ ~
can you hear the lion's ravenous roar?
The moan and groan of hunger to be appeased,
carnal need to feel just one more sacrifice desired
by the lioness beast who is part woman born,
with the wings of a bird and serpent's lashing tail.

She slides with silent grace through dark of night
seeing another victim walking the trail of shadows.
The she-beast whispers into his unsuspecting ear,
"Which creature in the morning goes on four feet,
at noon on two, and in the evening upon three?"
The riddle left unanswered, his heart belonged to her.

Soft fingers that caress like silken threads,
hands of a strangler flexed with brutish strength,
she revels in the power of one more conquest met.

Her magical beauty used to mesmerize and enchant,
demonic appetite thus sated with but one more
devoured soul, fresh taste of blood upon sweet lips.

In her twitching ears a fading beat from a dying heart,
consumed by human frailties, deceit and lies.
Roaring at a golden, resplendent moon she unwrapped
her wings, soaring into darkened sky towards the morn
of another approaching blood-red and tangerine sunrise,
her urgent desires satisfied, her hunger now subdued.
Gliding upon angry thermals, long wings spread wide,
sinister shadows brushed a shivering earth below.
Night after night her lion roared as death begets
more death, souls once lost upon the living now
within her chants the song of everlasting life,
for she is the Queen of Darkness, Demon of Destruction.

Came that fateful night she asked the question,
"Which creature in the morning goes on four feet,
at noon on two, and in the evening upon three?"
Oedipus smiled for he knew the answer to destroy her.
"Man - who crawls on all fours as a baby, then walks
on two feet as an adult, and with a cane in his old age."

With a painful growl that rumbled across the ground,
an angry roar that thundered though the heavens,
and a shriek that stilled all human heartbeats,
the she-beast cast her body from a ragged cliff,
the demon now devoured by lost souls within her ~ ~
terrifying night of the Sphinx to be no more.

~ ❈ ~ ❈ ~ ❈ ~

Yet still, when silvered moon hangs high
and dark breath of night caresses me,
the growl starts low within my breasts.
Wild lion craves to stalk the streets
and raptor shrieks to flee the nest.
The demon beast will rule once more
for someone this night will surely die.

The Fog

It's such an ominously surreal world,
lost within this mysterious fog.
I wade through hungry tendrils a' swirl
around a sense of apprehension
and a very curious dog.

~ ~ ~ ~ ~

So creepy,
eerily strange,
darkly alien,
a landscape for the deranged.

~ ~ ~ ~ ~

Stagnant air so deathly disturbing
that I can hear whispers from arousing flowers
mingle with the anxious chirping
of stretching, early-morning browsers.

~ ~ ~ ~ ~

Lost amid this realm of sin,
a shroud of pallid gray
tickles my skin,
beseeching arrival of a burgeoning day.

~ ~ ~ ~ ~

Frightened eyes
peer into a dense curtain
of insistent and breathless sighs,
my anguished thoughts of you uncertain.

~ ~ ~ ~ ~

An arrogant owl hoots alone.
I swear it called out your name.
Or maybe not ~ just a painful moan,
a morning song of beckoning rain.

~ ~ ~ ~ ~

As we walk, the fog lifts its gaze
through glistening leaves towards the sun.
This alien terrain now awash in a golden haze,
eyes staring through tears for my special someone.

The Gatekeeper

~ ~ Darkness looms ~ ~

on broken brow, my tragic soul
hath long departed, no longer me
with body drained of all life sustaining
organs. Thin shaft of light, so deadly bright,
reveals a Door ~ the Gate ajar ~ a Portal to
dark Underworld, black eyes of death
now sordid bound, devoid of love
upon whispered tears amid
heartless scorn, this sad
and broken life afloat
on water red, ahead
the tombs of ~ ~

~ ANUBIS ~

Lord of the Dead,
the Keeper of the Gate,
the path to Cyonopolis *City
of the Dogs* his breasts the form
of woman born, as the head of Jackal
grins and leers with hooded eyes of pity.
I gazed through shades of fear, seeing bodies
spread on icy slabs of stone, sharp blade of blood
within his hands, now soul released to float away
upon a dark River of the Dead, once human
shell now filled up by the Embalmer,
sweet Guardian of the Veil.

~ ~ ANUBIS ~

the God of Dying,
our Patron of Lost Souls and
Orphans, awesome Lord of the Dead.
As I float away to who knows where, I see
my heart placed with loving care upon the scale
to be measured with the feather, praying that my heart
is light and presented to Osiris, for if the heart be
heavy, then the horrid mouth of Ammit doth
open wide, crocodile teeth with the hiss
of cat thus devours the soul I once
possessed amid the screams in
the Hall of Two Truths.

Upon the Throne
in darkened veil sits Thoth,
frightening Prosecutor of the Dead,
while Osiris looks on upon the final court,
this judge that will determine if my deeds within
this life were good enough to be lighter than the feather
of Ma'at, Goddess of Truth. I try and hold my breath
of which I have no more, worried that my heart
be too heavy as my soul will be devoured.
Osiris stands with arms spread wide,
The feather has not moved. My
soul thus saved and now held
within the dark hands of

~ ANUBUS ~

Kiss of the Black Rose

Maddening in its starkness,
I stared at an immense, darkly ornate door,
deathly afraid to push it open and reveal what was inside.
Frightened at what might be in store,
going from salvation's light to wicked darkness,
my manic thoughts cried from beyond the graveside.

But push in the door I did.
With an ominous squeak that rang
throughout the empty corridors of my existence,
I peered into screaming shadows before I slide
within, the angry door slamming shut with a bang.
My anxious heart pounded madly with foreboding resistance.

In the center of the room stood a monstrous table,
a long, desolate, silent slab of wood
over which a lonely light bulb cast its eerie glow.
I slowly stepped forward, nearly unable
to stop my nervous hands from shaking, aware I would
be too unstable to reach for a hushed, black rose.

For I could see, lying upon this austere surface,
eight black roses which seemed to breathe
with a vibrant resonance all their own.
There was one in particular that cried
out my name, incredibly seeming to seethe
with the plangent chime of a prognostic metronome.

My fingertips caressed one of the beautiful, black flowers.
Suddenly, it jumped onto my palm, skin ablaze,
my startled eyes squeezing shut in pain.

A sharp, angry, lacerating shaft of light devoured
all my fears, incinerating broken yesterdays.
Then the rose whispered your name.

In shock, I backed against the door in fear.
A mist appeared from shadows that held your eyes,
then your face, and seconds later, your arms reaching for me.
I stared down at the rose and saw one tear.
"Worry not, for you will be together again," it sighed.
You smiled as your vision faded, my heart beating thankfully.

I quietly left the room to its stunning silence, for
upon the table still rested fourteen black roses, awaiting compliance.

Anita Gates

I have always wanted to write and always known that one day I really could and would. I have met many wonderful people who have helped me to grow as a writer, given me so much confidence in my own ability to be able to express myself through written words. Poetry, art and music mean so much to me. I love words, to mold them at my own will and to give a glimpse of myself to others. Lately I have been thinking about writing several short stories for a little project. I currently study psychology and I also have a Certificate of Natural Sciences at University level. I am very proud and awed to be a member of this special group and grateful for all the encouragement I get here.

Angels

I can
feel
the wind
of
angels'
wings

It gives
Me
Hope for
All those
Things.

I can
Hear
Angels
Silently
Whispering,

I can
Feel
Them
Around me
Shimmering.

Golden dust
On rainbows,
A faded memory
Of a pale rose.
I'm a jaded soul...

Passing on in Soft Voice

Without the Sun I'm silent
I strived for the best
Through my own faults
My word was my bond,
I am not lost
Not all of me will die,
Do not pursue
Our sorrowful sea,
Save me and I'll save you
Remember the guilt
Music soothes the savage beast ~

Skates Hung on the Wall

As stars' pure light glisten on white velvet ice
Like broken fragments of diamonds in disguise
She kneels and puts a palm to touch the sheet of cold
And the ancient memories fill the minds void.

Her bowed head mourns a distant past
Not willing to let it fade to fast...
Behind closed eyes doors open, flooding her with delight
She lingers in this illusion to strengthen her weak fight

A solemn vow to herself stands in her sorrow's way
Never to allow beauty or love in herself to decay
Sadness creeps upon her with a strangle-grip on belief
As she reaches and cradles her clutches of maimed relief.

Death's Lullaby

This lucid radiance
Unfolds the image of the effervescent air
Upon which the rippling light is breaking,
Your suffusing gaze
Crown the night.
With glowing skin
You give me back my phantom love.
And a dark canopy of senses line
Your fading lips...~

The Boy

He turns to face
The darkest demons and deepest shadows
His soul longs for a world
Where he could find peace in understanding
His soulful, quiet mourning
For the loss of everything that's important
Echoes in your mind
He was born under the wrong moon
But strong as the ocean
And pure as falling rain
He stands defiant
Against the fear sweeping
The desert of his soul
In a world of solitude
Everything obeys the rules
Of an ephemeral life
And beauty is a slave to abide
The sounds of his beating heart
That ricochet across the emptiness
Of mind are his only nemeses
That bring comfort
To purify the sublime touch of
Fate's subdued hands
His eternal eyes hold
Love restrained and
No expectations
To enslave...

~

Sylvia's World

The girl in the mirror
Smiled with both eyes
Darkly,
Through the glass
Her voice creamy
And so willing
To let the cold storm within
to die

Outside
all is quiescent
I hear the silence bent
As the moon's sculpting
The nightscape
With silver light
Iridescent
Her words
raining on me
from the darkest skies
deep in myself

She offers me God
To keep as my
Panacea
And once again
I incur the blurred shapes
Fading without light
She wants the tears to end
In her eyes

Bright softness flashes
As she hunts for the light
Behind these eyelashes

Each moment breathing
A putative meaning
Of what's real and what's not
Seemingly unrestorable
Peace
So erased by angst
Instills solitude in me
The absence forced
To lift my face
And a sole memory edges near
To brace apace

You will never know
The color of liquid fear
And I will not be left
To beg for your kindness

This attic have seen
Rivers of tears
To flow under the skin
Invites you to repose
But only plays music to the dead bones
All alone now
White crow...
As night enclosed her fragile life
Life's prayer
Became
Death's innate fire
So commit it to the flames
My rose's death trickling

From the eyes of pain itself
Arising bluntly
And I stand before her
With this newly purified belief
That nothing comes from nothing
And that we too are stardust
As she disappears
In to light untouched
~

Gauche Masquerade

Do you really believe that you can magic away
These sore tears indefinitely?

And that we can continue
On the gondola of life unseen?
I am insatiable to know...

Your gaze upon me is rebirth
Each time pioneers new emotions
How odd they would never return
Your arms, my hearse
They'll take away
This unrest in me
This labyrinth we've been through
Paved with orchids of all color
Disrobed our naked intentions
A lifetime of solitude couldn't make me
Forget these things

Touch that rips the my garment of sorrow
And what's underneath is hemmed in lace
Voice that soothes severed faith
As you observe with care
The field of concealed dark tears
You kill the torment of discarded feelings
That mar 'till I'm too weak to breathe

And when you're hurt in the amalgam
Of flora and night bloom
A small part of me dies each time
In the pouring rain

As pain clutches at your tender spirit
You summon laughter to fill in gaping holes
That run deep in drab eves
And I capture your castle
Whilst walking in sand bare feet
The tiny bell
In the centre of this heart's
Hidden niche
Flutters and dances elated
Aching no more
Settled and tamed
As falling autumn leaf
The forbidden arch of magenta lips
Bring me closer
To toss aside

This monsters' ball
behind my gauche masquerade~

Immaculate

Some things will never change...

The swing she used to sit on
Feet lightly moving
Wondering, remembering
As the clouds wept endlessly

Her antique memories are engraved
With symbols of life and death
And inner eyes of yesteryears
Dive into dreams unfed

A door opening onto darksome reflections...

"The orchid-sweet taste of your lips
will always stay with me
The scent of rain on your alabaster skin
Will never leave me
The filed of innocence of your eyes
Would haunt me 'till the end of times

Her insignificant death stains
The stealing beauty of silver snow
Dispels blinding screams
Her only legacies
Descended realizations of knowing
That from now on
Distant stars will illuminate
Her darkening sky
In a place where her spirit can truly play
Thus all impurity

Silently enfolded
Within others' vast longing

Listen
To the newly fallen round snow drops

Listen
To the stealthy power of woven sadness
Echoing through the stillness of air
Awaiting to be boundless in happiness

Her lingering memory is placed to rest
With cold powder in scooped hands
Over her white pillowed head
In that deep velvet green dress

The snow falls heavy
Over her immaculate grave
And a lone soul breathes ever so gently
~

Coyote Ravin

I imagined darkness more
Weightless
Where eyes echo nothing
Where angels
Lull time into sleep
Each saying
' I'll keep remembering '

the hunter's unmade dreams
you bring
and I see you howl like coyotes
your essence flutters by
like a butterfly
as through stained glass
light makes visible dust
but your breath carries a chill
that makes
black bones shiver in disgrace

I used to bare myself
Right before you
Unburdening
Porcelain beads of me
Carefully
As you proceeded
To harvest Vega's beauty
Behind your chest
A heart-shaped box
It's secrets once falling on me
As I pleaded
'Rock me gently

when the nightmares come
and if I should die
I want to die inside your kiss'

We have a history and it's ancient
Full of fossils of memories
I remember the whispering trees
Or sailing on a flow of crystal light
Wavering
But it's all passed do you hear?
And I am just a harpy of your penal colony
'I count moments
upon your return'
I lie
Because it is torture
The songs of Sonoran
Now just a dirge hauled by time

Rain collects
In your cupped hands
From startled eyes
Look down and see the pain reflect
As you reap kindness
Watchfully

The coyotes bow to me
As you weep wily
And I kiss your eyelids
Lightly

Fragments of Truths

You see there?...just over there?...
...how the globe of Venus burns with red anger?

The moment you lost the shine
to that sexy attitude (fast declined)
I spiraled right out of your control...
you acted like I was the bait
hauling me in contentedly
and I stepped into a casket full of mistakes
toiling with dreams...

Each look in these eyes learnt
that the grave truths are found under
the pebbles of what's remembered...
A beaten fay
with heart pounded on the anvil
climbing a mountain of waste
all fazed
as the gleaming amulet
falls to the ground from around my neck...

The crescent of the night played away
in drops of miracles
in a cradle of sugar for plastic lovers
touch born of known hands
hands born of thrills
fingertips coddle unswept hips
with the sweetness of tubular bells....
but the love in me is a little wary of you
with surprise and disbelief akin
and I don't really want to preach anymore you see...

It's late...
and I reckon it's time to leave
calm hands reach to the wall
to gently lift and unsheathe
this old Katana sword
with its double-bladed silver edges
turned towards me...

I see my cold reflection in it
and tighten my grip on its hilt...

Nevermore

...and I slip away
under the cupola
of a prismal night
I, your transparent talisman
a gliding breath
through the spirit of death...

Alas, I am now only
a whisper, a lullaby and
I won't wake again
but don't you cry
as my dark swan
fades in to the last cusp
of the red sun
darkness awaits to entwine
the ruins of a nevermore soul
with the stilled winds of the shadows...

A sinner sobbing in angelic candor
tonight be not the one
who is christened by fire and blood
as rain drips onto the cross
I lay to rest my pain and sadness
in paradise lost
with unclenched hands
unafraid within the star-studded armor of love
unscarred with pale absolution illuminating
a nevermore touch...

Don't you weep...
look for me on the edge
of a pastel moon's halo
in the color of butterflies
beautifying an empty world
look for me in dreams
yet undreamt
in the veins of fallen
autumn leaves dressed in cold earth
look for my flickering light
in the deep shadows birthed by the night
in the simple motion of knowing hands
and the taste of salty tears that fall but never end

See me in the epigraph
of sunrise and moonsets
sleeping upon your dreams
as I wipe away a nevermore kiss
see me in the airy pattern of dust
where I've hidden stood
in the mirror of your face for so long
that you have never understood...

Don't you weep...
look for me on the edge
of a pastel moon's halo
in the color of butterflies
beautifying an empty world
look for me in dreams
yet undreamt
in the veins of falen
autumn leaves dressed in cold earth
look for my flickering light
in the deep shadows birthed by the night

in the simple motion of knowing hands
and the taste of salty tears that fall but never end

See me in the epigraph
of sunrise and moonsets
sleeping upon your dreams
as i wipe away a nevermore kiss
see me in the airy pattern of dust
where i 've hidden stood
in the mirror of your face for so long
that you have never understood...

Angelic Asylum

I have become dark
and so broken in your reality,
an angel on dead wings
no longer unseen...
in a perfect circle
of rebirth in silence
left to listen to my own suffering

The passing guilt salutes me
but I still wear the imprint of hate
on the inside of my soul...
defeated I start a new battle
and I no longer care
for the runes carved by blood
into the white walls closing in
beneath the howling
and I find not one thing
to rip the pain out

Without a mask
I witness the embrace of submission
and that love with its metamorphic spell
is only a necromantic wonder
drowned in a sea of ashes
in the harrowing flow of life

Dusk lays me down dying
lets the dense night fall upon me
lets the black earth become my face
as nothing fights for me in a haste

lending me the knowledge:
in darkness there is no fear...

The footsteps of Death
already etched on my forehead...

H. Brian Damon II

I must say that writing to me, is a great way of expressing my ideas and opinions of the way I see things. Life is like a giant prism everyone sees it through a different color and or angle. I view life from a darker angle and my writing tends to reflect that part of my nature, yet I find that depending upon my Muse, I can and have written about things from a lighter side. So sit back and enjoy the journey to the dark side. One more thing, Patti Hearsey (my English composition teacher sophomore year of high school) wherever you are thank you for pushing me to write and not using that damn red ink pen on my papers.

The Black Rose Poets Society, I don't know that I will ever be able to thank them enough. Since my acceptance into this exclusive group of writers I have watched my writing grow. We continue to push each other to the limits and beyond so our writing is and will always be the best it can be. It is an honor to have been chosen to be a part of this anthology, and I consider all of the members to be my friends.

His Own Suicide

Driving the knife deep into his chest
Eyes rolling back in ecstasy
Fill it rising within the throat
Bile from a churning stomach
Blood spills to the ground
Staining all that it touches
Bloodied fingers grip the knife
Waves of pleasure course the spine
Pull it out only to drive it in again
Piercing skin, cutting bone, nature of the beast
Quivering inhalation of sweat tinged air
The smell of fear driving him on
Watching as blood pours from his mouth
Punctured lung, the Reaper is calling
Blood pooling at his feet
Weakened knees begin shake
Determined step forward
To confront this unknown
Shock spreads across his face
In agonizing horror
Realization of a new threat
Dawns as the life blood drains
Lack of understanding
The why or the how
Do not matter now
Death is looming at the door
It knocks once, twice, thrice
Cold touch upon his soul
As he looks into the mirror
Seeing his own suicide
Releasing the bloodied knife

Clanging to the floor
Eyes rolling back into his head
Sliding to the floor
Unconscious life's blood pours
The Reaper smiles
Swinging his scythe
Raping the soul
While he carries it
To eternal Hell

Demon in the Priest

In nomine dei nostri satanas luciferi excelsi
Exclaims the young man in the center of a pentagram
Five black candles one at each point of the white star
Go out as one followed by an eerie silence
The young man is picked up and slammed face down
Blood red stains the center of the once white star
The walls of the room burst into flames
The young man finds himself at the foot
Of Satan's alabaster throne of bones
The young man looks nervously around
I have invoked you Satan
And I desire your possession of my soul
Make me a leader of men
Charismatic so that all who hear will believe
Knowledge of the black art so I may work magik
And your presence in my mind always
Upon hearing this Satan stands
Spreading his wings Satan transforms his body
A dragon like figure stands before the young man
Satan in dragon form reaches through
The large scale covering his breast
And pulls out half of his heart
Dripping blood with its rhythmic beat
Held in Satan's hand he steps to the young man
And thrusts it into his chest
Pain as blood burns with fire
Agony as it spreads through out his body
The young man screams as Satan laughs
You shall always feel my presence
You are my High Priest and founder now
Return to Earth and build me a church

An empire to rival that of the Vatican
Your symbol will be the Baphomet
And you will call it the Church of Satan
The year is 1966
Many years later it is still growing
Even after the death of its founder

Psychosis in a Padded Cell

Wandering thoughts
Falling into darkness
Fleeting glimpses of Life
Needle pierces skin
Drug induced psychosis
Straight-Jacketed arms
Flail to no avail
Padded walls surround
Deafening silence prevails
Surrendering to insanity
Watching in timelessness
As the paint peels off the walls
Reality out of reach
Cold touch upon the mind
Inner demon speaks
"Within these walls
Turmoil prevails"
Bruised alter-ego
Beaten down by time
Locked within these padded walls
Longing for freedom
That will never come
Suppressed by medicine
The true personality
Is slowly forgotten
Many years later
A shell of the man
He once was is
Left lying on the floor
Shivering from fear
Of the voices
Heard from the walls
Painfully surrounded by
Wandering thoughts

Lord of Dark Delusions

From the depths of the misguided mind
I have come, to pray upon your soul
The twisted and perverse tremble in my wake
For I am The Lord of Dark Delusions

Psychotic atrophy in a macabre mind
Tormenting and tearing at your fragile being
Reveling in your fear and pain I caused
I am the Lord of Dark Delusions

I am a godless entity cursed to forever roam
Taking out my vengeance on the weak
Simple minded fools that populate my memories
I am the Lord of Dark Delusions

Showing a mother her dead child in a dream
Slaughtered before her eyes
Watch as she cries and moans in her sleep
I am the Lord of Dark Delusions

Watching as the Father prays for mercy
While I cause hallucinations of grandeur
And destroy his dreams and wishes
I am the Lord of Dark Delusions

Showing the gleaming blade to the suicidal child
Laughing as he cuts his veins and life blood pours
Feeding off of his fear as he realizes he is going to die
I am the Lord of Dark Delusions

Hand in hand with the Queen of the Damned
Walking the earth bringing fear and torment
Fulfilling the need to darken another day
For I am the Lord of Dark Delusions

If I am Screaming

Please don't wake me if I am screaming
Left to my own demise might have some meaning
Wandering visions of unprovoked thoughts
Dancing through my brain

Clinical expressions of a life devoid
Muscles tensed, fist full of hair
Begin to pull
Pain, oh the wondrous pain

In a restless slumber of drug induced paranoia
Nightmares of demonic quality
Prey upon my godless soul
Racking my body with uncontrolled spasms

Taking the knife, feeling the forged steel
As it runs across my flesh
Seeing the blood as it pools upon the floor
Wanting and needing the pain once more
Sick and twisted in my perversion
I let the blade fall to the floor

Seeing a message with in my pooled blood
I get down on my hands and knees
For a closer look.
Above the puddles of blood staring intently
I fail to see the hands

The hands from another dimension
Reaching through the floor, viciously
Latching onto my arms and pulling
Straight through the floor I fall.

A gothic nightmare straight from hell
Blood curdling screams escape my mouth
As I realize my destination
The finality of it chills my bones

The Reaper has come to collect my debt
I sold my soul, for love, long ago
You cant wake me now even if I am screaming
Left to my own demise does have some meaning

Shadow of the Harvester

Fog swirling between the stones, of a barren waste land
Fleeting glimpses, of an unknown entity
Walking through this land of death, feelings abound
Cold and clammy skin, Forebode a chilling tale
Lessons taught to children, of the Shadow called the Harvester
Unknown from whence it came, the Harvester searches
For children lost in nightmares, having not a corporeal body
He slides into and out of dreams like a spider
Once tangled in his web, a child is said forever lost
An empty but living shell remains, shattered by unspeakable horrors
In a mind boggling nightmare, A labyrinth of epic proportions
Forms from the Harvester's web, For freedom the center must be reached
The loss of innocence, has now begun
A subtle soaking mist falls, as the shadows of previous children
Surround the newest victim, of the Harvester's Labyrinth
Covering their faces, with transparent hands
To hide the giggle, as they all point, each in a different direction
Twisting and turning, climbing and descending
Searching what feels like forever, for the ultimate goal
The center of this nightmarish maze
Through trials of fear, tests of courage, and temptations of the soul
The harvester tries to prevent, the release from his grasp
A Minotaur guarding, a doorway through which you must pass
Challenges you to a duel of brute strength, a fight to the death
With acceptance he charges, head lowered horns leading
Quickly backing to the wall, small and lithe
The child climbs, as the Minotaur slams into the wall beneath
Breaking his neck, with dying breath he says "You have won your passage"
Passages and tunnels, bridges and swings
Traversing through the Labyrinth

Pushing onward, ever towards the prize, freedom from
This nightmare of tangled webs and deceit
Candies and cookies unfold before this child
Tempting and daring, to stay and eat just one
Promising satisfaction, and a never ending supply
With the aroma of the sweets, the ruble of a stomach
Brings back reality, determined to win, turns and walks away

No child has ever made it past the temptation of the sweets
Howling in anger, the Harvester swears while looking through
His crystal ball as unfolding events reveal the foretelling of his demise
Pushing onward, closer and closer, the center of the Labyrinth looms
A spire of Basalt marks absolute center, carved within this stone
Are the names, names of the lost children, cursed to forever roam
The child reaches out and touches the spire
"I have survived your maze, now I demand my release"
From behind the spire the Harvester speaks
"Nay my child, you have reached the center
But one more test of great importance is required

Are you willing to stay within the confines of this Labyrinth
To release, those before you back to their Mothers"
Pictures of Mother and Father fly through the child's thoughts
Visions of happiness, times of wonder and of sadness
The gentle touch of Mother, callused hand of Father
Longing to return to them, the child turns and looks
Seeing the hundreds of shadows, from the victims of the Harvester
The child speaks, "I have the courage to face you alone, release them"
One by one the shadow children begin to fade, traveling back to their bodies
With the departure of each and every child's shadow
The Harvester grows thinner, until all that remained was the one
Who made it to the center to bring about his demise
Trembling in fear the once powerful Harvester awaits
Turning his attention back to the quivering shadow at his feet

The child says, "I no longer believe in you"
With the words uttered from the mouth of a babe
The Harvester slowly fades and is no more
The Labyrinth begins to crumble and the webs of deceit
Start to snap weakening the fabric of its creation
The child watches with a smile on his face
With the demolition complete the Labyrinth is gone
The Harvester destroyed, nightmares only nightmares again
Awakening with a jolt, the child looks around
With a deep breath the child rolls over, pulls the covers up
And goes back to sleep, to seek out and destroy
Another "Bogey Man" of the Shadows

Auschwitz

Loud banging upon the door
Middle of the starlit night
The SS has arrived to claim them
"Pack what you will in one bag"
Auschwitz
Standing room only in a box car
Railed through the country
Just because of their faith
Persecuted for their race
Auschwitz
Freezing cold murderous conditions
Children cry and the elderly wail
Hunger grips at their mind
As the thirst tears at their throats
Auschwitz
The rhythmic motion of the rail car
Begins to slow a gentle snow begins to fall
A funny smell assaults the nose
The death camp looms in the distance
Auschwitz
Under the tower of the main entrance
Slowing to a stop on the third track
The sliding door opens with
"Every one out"
Auschwitz
Freedom has finally arrived they thought
Slowly gathering into groups of friends
Stretching sore legs enjoying the fresh air
"Women and children to the left, Men to the right"
Auschwitz
The "ramp of death's final selection" has begun

Young women fit to work are spared momentarily
The elderly and too young are moved along
Unknowingly towards their deaths
Auschwitz
Final selection has begun for the men
Able bodied and over fourteen
Sent out for slave labor in the mine fields
While the unpicked are marched to the killing rooms
Auschwitz
Led to believe they are walking
Towards the family camps
The promise of a shower and hot meal
Fresh with in their minds
Auschwitz
The family is together once more save one
Father, mother, baby and small child
Eldest boy has been "picked" for the labor camps
All is well they think not knowing how close death is
Auschwitz
"We must wait for a moment to let the others join us"
Is what they hear as they enter a small copse of tree's
Sitting down children begin to play bringing smiles to mothers faces
Only one hundred feet from the building hidden by the trees
Auschwitz
Once all of the people have gathered
Over two thousand innocent souls
Do the SS allow them to move again
Breaking through the edge of the trees they see
Auschwitz
"This is your shower and meal
Half into this building half into the other"
Not wanting to miss either
The family hurriedly enters the building on the right
Auschwitz

Through the double doors and into a large open room
"Take off your clothing the water will come from the pipes
And you may shower before your meal" double doors lock
Undressing for the promised shower they wait for the water
Auschwitz
A terrible sounding hiss from the vents in the wall
Those closest begin to choke and gag
Grasping at their throats and eyes rolling back into their heads
Falling dead to the floor, everyone now knows it's
Auschwitz
Mothers holding their child up only to prolong its life
Mass hysteria locked into a room of hell and deadly gas
Begging for a reason why pleading for release
Crying to their God to forgive their captors
Auschwitz
One by one they all slowly and painfully die
After clearing out the gas they haul
The lifeless bodies to the crematoria
And the "snow" begins anew
Auschwitz
The eldest boy wonders what has happened
Has not seen his family for three days
Watching as the train pulls into the yard
And the disembarkation begins
Auschwitz
The "final selection" begins again
With interest the boy watches from a distance
As the biggest group is marched to the same place as his family
With a question he wishes was never answered he now knows
Auschwitz
The wail of a thousand voices permeates the air
As they are put to a horrible and senseless death
Mass murder in a gas chamber
All in the name of racial purity

Auschwitz
Hitler in his grand design of
Blonde haired, blue eyed Aryans
Was not, but descended from
Questionable genealogy
Auschwitz
No tombstone to mark their graves
Just a hole in the ground filled with ash
All mothers, Fathers and children
Lost souls cursed to forever roam
Auschwitz

Dead Hollow Cemetery

As you walk up to the rusted gates
A chill courses through your spine
Dark and damp in a fog covered night
You read the sign "Dead Hollow Cemetery"
With racing mind you go over the events
The creation of your journey four hours ago
"I am the man" and "Nothing scares me" you stated
Not able to back down you accepted your fate
Spend one night alone in Dead Hollow Cemetery
A slight breeze stirs the fog at your feet
And rustles through the trees before you
As you walk into the cemetery
The feelings begin
Your senses are assaulted with the unknown
Hearing everything and nothing all at once
Catching movement at the corner of your eye
Quickly turning you see a cloaked and hooded figure
walking away from you towards the center
of Dead Hollow Cemetery
Quietly following wondering what is up
You see another figure approaching and then another
Stopping you count nine in all
They reach the clearing in the center of the cemetery
With the wave of a hand
The first figure starts a raging fire
Shadows dance across tombstones and trees
Playing tricks with your mind in the swirling fog
You would swear demons danced in those flames
The Nine form a circle and begin a chant
Unknown to you the chant is Enochian
The archaic language of Angels long ago

Not able to tell what is said
You begin to feel a creeping dread
The wind in the trees rustling the leaves
Sound as if a thousand souls were whispering at once
To scared to move for fear of disruption
You stay rooted to the spot
The chanting has now stopped
The silence of the night is deafening
An evil arcane voice pierces the night
"Charon the escort of dead souls,
Lucifer Lord over the all the lustful,
Cerebus torturer of the gluttons,
Plutus wolf like demon of the wealthy,
Beelzebub harbinger of the wrathful,
Belail ruler of the city of Dis and destroyer of heretics,
Devil overseer of the tyrants and war-mongers
Abaddon the horned demon whipping the hypocrites
And I, I am the fallen one
Satan the king of Cocytus and all nine levels of Hell."
Hearing this decree your knees buckle
As you fall to your knees you see
The faces of The Nine looking at you
Frozen in place like an animal in headlights
The Nine slowly float towards you.
The stench of fear soaked sweat
Pours from your body enticing The Nine
You are slowly surrounded your terror builds
Laughing Satan spreads his wings out of the cloak
Steps forward and reaches out towards you
As all the stories, fears and evil terrors
Flow through your mind you loose consciousness
Darkness and silence surround you now
Time has stood still with no way to know
As you push through your clouded brain to conscious

You are now laying on a stone altar with binded limbs
Surrounded by The Nine your horror begins
Abaddon looks at you and states scornfully
"I am the man, Nothing scares me you hypocrite
Preaching fearlessness yet fainting at our sight
You now belong to me"
Abaddon slowly pulls down the hood covering his face
As the cloth falls around his neck you recoil in shock
Two great horns protrude from his head
Flowing like a serpent down his neck
To curl towards his chin and around again
To his ears a full circle gleaming black and red
"For your sin this night you are bound to Hell
Eternal darkness for the Malebolge is your fate
Say your goodbyes human in a fortnight you are mine"
Then Abaddon pierces your chest with a silver clave
And thus you are marked
You awaken with the sun in your eyes
Looking around you see the tombstones
Awakening your fears at the sight of your epitaph
You flee Dead Hollow Cemetery
Telling your tale none believe you
Smiling and laughing they refuse your goodbyes
Now fourteen days later your body is found
The cause of death unknown no marks on your body
Save one smoking trident brand on your neck
Your family and friends all cry as they decide
You are to be interned in the earth at
Dead Hollow Cemetery

The Storm

Lazily drifting to the ground
The snow begins to fall
Softly caressing the trees
From the tip to the base
Upon this mountain top
Undisturbed silence abounds
While the snow blankets the ground
The mountain is hidden by the clouds
Obscuring the sight
Of the storm that hits tonight

Building a fury of wind and snow
Carried by a fierce Nor' Eastern Gale
The storm advances onward
Marching with its own rhythm
Towards a thunder head
Out of the South West
The battle for supremacy
Will be fought
When the two heavy weights collide
Over the top of the Mountain

In the valley below the Mountain
Lightning strike, Thunder clap
The rain begins
Steadily pouring down
Beating the grass into the ground
Rolling Thunder echoes
And Lightning strikes
Mark the movement

Of the Thunder head
Towards the mountain

The snow falls faster now
Breaking the silence
That it had blanketed
Only hours before
The steady pattering
As it hits the ground
Creates a staccato of sound
With the creaking of the trees
Telling a foreboding tale
Of the snow to come

The wind begins
Whipping up the mountain
Slicing through the trees
Tearing at the bushes
Pushing the snow into a flurry
Spinning the icy shards
Out of control
Drifts begin on the leeward sides
Creating deep voids of piled snow
As the wind rages on

Snapping of tree limbs
As the weight of the snow
Bends them towards the ground
The slow but gentle crush
Of the under brush
As the snow deepens
The collision of the storms
Has created a blizzard

The likes of which
Have never been seen

The fury of the mega storm
Fed by the two giants
Rages through most of the night
With the cresting of the Sun
On the Eastern horizon
Light slowly climbs
Up the side of the mountain
Revealing a stunning vista
Shining like a diamond
At the head of the Valley

The amounts of snow
Immeasurable
Once majestic Evergreens
Buried all save the tallest ones
The silent lucidity
Of the snow storm
Destruction in pure form
Until it melts away and is gone
Hides its damage from prying eyes
Under a pristine blanket of white

Of a Life Torn

Within the darkness it crawls
Illuminated by a witches candle
Along a twisting path
Paved with the broken promises
Of a life torn
Illusions of grandeur
Twirl through thoughts
Like a skirt on a dancing stick
Of pigtails and red ribbon
A necessary evil
Lumination's from the night light
Play across the walls
Painting pictures no one should see alone
Pounding of the heart as the fear is rising
Watching it as it grows
The plunger is pulled back
Sucking in the smack
Of a fifty lick hit
Swearing this is the last
Knowing you cant change the past
Within the darkness it crawls
Tearing down defenseless walls
Placing another brick on the path
Paved with the broken promises
Of a life torn

Carol Digou

Poetry has been a means of emotional expression for members of my family for generations. My mother and grandmother were poets. My son is a songwriter and musician, and uses his talent to work for environmental and social causes. My daughter is also a poet and a nature photographer. Much of my work deals with the environment, social commentaries, or things of an inner spiritual nature. I am not religious, in that I reject organized religions and most of what they stand for. I am, however, highly spiritual and that colors everything I write in some way.

My life has been filled with many intense events that have molded my views and perspectives. Nearly all of my writing comes from something very specific in my life experience, but I try to write in such a way that each reader can easily apply his or her own interpretation. I believe the language of poetry and music is universal, and that words spoken in this language may be heard where others fall on deaf ears. I also believe that one must understand the dark to find the light, and that to be truly whole one must be aware of both and must find the balance between the two. My first full book of poetry, "Elemental Expression", can be purchased at Amazon, Barnes and Noble, and other on line book stores.

I am proud to be a member and President of the Black Rose Poets' Society and to share poetic growth with such a talented and multi-faceted group.

Metamorphosis

Blackness surrounded him like a soft velvet cloak,
Soothing him with nothingness.
Feeling weightless and without perspective,
He allowed himself to float.
Silence soothed his sapless soul,
Fluffing the quilt of darkness that wrapped him.
Looking inward, he reached outward,
Feeling himself disperse and expand.
The soothing dark caressed him
With the freedom of nothingness.
And as he drifted thinly through invisible space,
He was warmed and gathered,
Pulled back, regaining form,
And the warmth began to glow,
Then expanded in a flashing light,
As he burst from his velvet veil
And emerged glowing with being anew,
Feeling whole and filled,
With a ball of darkness in his left hand,
And one of light in his right.

Vigilante

Night slammed down like the trunk of a 1940 Buick.
I stretched and started my prowl...
A tomcat surveying his perimeter,
A hunter - hunting the hunters.

They were out there.
The scum of society,
Feeding on the lives of the innocent,
Dirtbags who were born without a conscience
Or who lost it so early
There was no memory left to fall back on.
Predators with no humanity
Left loose to victimize
And no one able to catch them...

That was my job.

I glided down the filthy sidewalk,
Stepping over broken bottles,
Navigating through waves of scattered garbage,
Under the burnt out street lights
That guide and protect no one.

Passing by several homeless,
Bundled up for the night under filthy, torn blankets
In a cardboard lean-to,
I heard a dog in the distance
Barking for a response
That would tell him he wasn't alone.

Junkies stood around an oil drum
Warming their hands on the fire
Built with combustible garbage
And old newspapers covered in vomit

Retrieved from the dumpster
Behind the sleazy bar across the street.

In an alley nearby was the noise
Of two tomcats (the four legged ones)
Deciding whose territory they were in.
Sirens in the distance
Sang of someone being rushed to the E.R.
They somehow sounded different
Than the ones on the cop cars
When they rushed to help
In a neighborhood safe enough
For them to get out alive.

Hookers huddled in groups,
Clustered for some semblance of safety.
None would last long...
Disease, drugs or death would catch them soon.

Three shots rang out in the silence of the night,
Rapid and deadly, followed by fleeing footsteps.
My guess was a gang dispute
Over turf that no one would want to own...
Big tomcats doing the same as the little ones.

And then I heard what I came for...
A muffled cry,
The sound of a garbage can being kicked aside,
Not far ahead.
My pace quickened, as my instincts went on full alert.
Stealth and familiarity are my allies.
Two alleys away I found them.
Two punks, one with a knife, one with a gun.
Tearing the worn clothes
From a late night waitress,

Knife at her throat, gun to her head,
Promising if she "cooperated" she would live.

She would be another statistic in the morning.
Found dead by the first junkie to slip down the alley,
The lying punks would kill her
Cooperation or not,
After they raped and beat her
To their satisfaction.

But not this night.
They were predators, but I was a bigger one.
They were hunters, but I had a mission.

Ski mask pulled down, swiftly, I moved in,
Asking no questions, giving no warning,
My Glock 19 in hand.
Two quiet pops.
Two dead punks.
Two less scumbags to terrorize.

I calmed the girl,
Walked her the four blocks
To the relative safety of her run-down apartment,
Lit a cigarette and faded off
Into the black of the night
With a satisfied smirk.
One more night,
Two more down,
God knows how many to go.

Venus (Fly-trap)

Form of a goddess,
Voluptuous and ripe,
Mutable with moods.
Chameleon who mirrors
Lusty thoughts and desires,
Able to please every taste.
Eyes like deep wells of azure,
Concealing the dry rot
At the bottom where no one sees.

Vacant soul, filled with chaos,
Obsessed with a self
That lacks in substance.
Running fast from a past
That lies a second behind.
Cursed with an empty hole,
An insatiable hunger to fill.
Stealing, taking, demanding,
Ravenous to flood the emptiness
With someone else's meaning.

She lures like a siren,
Vulnerable, exotic, erotic, neurotic,
Displaying the skin each victim seeks.
Like a magnet, she draws them,
Creator of fantasy, every man's dream.

Never hearing the warning,
Blinded by illusion and lust,
They march to her lair...
March to the rhythm
Of her swaying arms and hips.

And the hunger inside her
Consumes and devours,
Digesting their souls and their will,
Leaving them blubbering in pain
And drowning in guilt.
As she licks her lips
And desperately races away to fill
The emptiness that gnaws within.

Shadows of the Soul

Smokey shadows nudge the recesses of the mind,
Lingering visions of what might have been...
What talents lie dormant, yet unexplored,
In the corner of energy unexpended?
What horizons lie sleeping with no sun to rise?

Undeveloped shades, unable to grow to regrets
For lack of attention and substance,
Too immature to merit deep thought,
Yet harboring unlimited potential ignored.
Brushing introspection like a feather on a cheek.

Hovering in day dreams of deeds not done,
Of lives not lived, of songs not sung,
The cloudy mist is imperceptible, yet covers all,
Robbing the soul of the sigh of satisfaction
That is sought and never reached.

Introspect

The twisted workings of the mind
As it grapples for keys to secret doors
That lead to knowledge sensed
From places and times unseen.
Scrambled attempts to untangle
The web of experience from the confines
Of the inadequate consciousness.

In dreams, in secret thoughts and musings
It taps lightly on the window of awareness,
Waiting for the veil to lift,
Probing for some hint of enlightenment,
Some encouragement that eyes can see.
Nagging, hovering, whispering, pausing,
Provoking the sleeping shadows.

Each knot untangled brings forth
A new stream of light, a new realization.
Each moment of clarity illuminates a path
That leads to expansion.
Each dot connected, each puzzle solved,
Each knowing that comes unquestioned
Polishes rust from the key that unlocks
The door to the hidden mirror.

Hunger

Hungry soul
Grasping at the gnawing,
Reaching, Searching...
A puppy seeking pats
Of definition, of existence...
Butterfly floating
Through amethyst sunset...
Bullet seeking target
To find meaning...
Vessel half empty
Desiring to be filled...

Longing, searching, clawing
For the other half that will
Combine, complete...
Trailing ribbons of thoughts
Tangled rivers of emotion
In a waterfall of words...
Swirling in a frenzy,
Still as a well,
Crying and dreaming
For the holy grail.

The still point touched
As the ocean of light
Engulfs and morphs...
Eyes of the mind
See immaturity in the search,
Revealing the prize
That lies within.

The hunger fades,
The blossom opens..
What was illusive and out of reach
Was always there inside...
The soul now full,
The blossom yields to the ripening fruit.

The Moment Between

Heat of summer's blazing sun
Follows its master, slowly sinking
Beneath the line of hiding
Below the edge of the jagged rocks.
Splashes of orange grasp
For final moments of glory,
Giving way to subtle hues of the evening.
Cooling air sends a breath of moisture
To parched and tired lands.
Amethyst clouds born of tangerine
Yield to indigo with last rays.

The moment between, the still point,
When day is no more and night is yet to come,
The moment when time no longer exists,
When reflection is without and within...
The moment of peace
In the purple mists of evening.

Message

You see me as a piece of molten rock
With growth for your use as a cover.
You are blind, my children.
For I am a living lifeship
With a delicate balance in my body,
Much like that of your own.
Would you sail in my azure seas
And drill holes in your boat?
Would you fly in my life-giving air
And cut off your wings?
Would you eat of my plentiful bounty
And poison your food?
No, you say...yet this is what you do.
Without me you are homeless.
If my health is destroyed
My body can not sustain you.
You are children...
Self serving,
Self gratifying,
Self indulging,
With no concept of the consequences.
I want to sustain you...
I want to nurture you...
But I will survive.
My instincts for self preservation
Will overcome my duty to you,
And I will allow you to self destruct.
Heed my warning
And let us heal each other
Before our time is ended together.

Watchful Eyes

Morning mist hovers gently
Over sage and pinions,
Leaving a hint of drink for a thirsty land.

Unseen eyes survey the scene,
Unseen hands reach out
To bless the living earth below.

Once they roamed freely,
Nourished by their respect
For that which they knew as Mother.

Once they were a part of the life
That played on the stage below,
That flourished beneath their now wistful eyes.

Once they fought and survived
And hunted and loved
And all was as it was meant to be.

Their way was lost to "progress",
Their life was taken by broken promises,
Stolen by intruders who conquered and caged.

All that remains is the struggling land,
The memories of the stones,
And the watchful eyes of the ghosts and shadows.

Song of the North

Flickering rainbow dancing through midnight sky,
Stars blinking in attempts to be noticed
Through the hypnotic array of alien colors.
He stands on the snowy hilltop
Making love to the magic that surrounds.

A long, haunting note is accompanied by the crackling
In the kaleidescope that swirls above.
A song of freedom, of independence, of celebration..
Hypnotic, mysterious, forlorn,
Filled with majesty and strength.
Joined by harmonious notes, the chorus begins,
Steady serenades in the background
With a staccato ballet weaving in and out.

Brittle cold hangs heavy in the clear of the night,
Ignored by the energy of life that defies it.
White world of whirling lights and swirling snows,
The timeless scene is one of dreams and visions
As the pack pours its soul into notes
That write the poetry of the wild.

From Far Away

Senseless wars ravage on
As leaders feed greed and lust for power.
Honorable sons fed faerie tales
Of reasons to march to their deaths.

Riches of indulgence are squandered
While on streets below
Children beg for crusts
While mothers prostitute their dreams,
Elders breathe their last breath
Under cardboard shields,
The promise of the young
Is eaten by a needle in the vein,
And would be survivors kill for a coin.

Famine sweeps across lands
Like a steady and unrelenting wind,
Leaving distended bellies,
Protruding bones and vacant eyes,
Hosting souls without hope.

Fear of damnation,
Fear of starvation,
Fear of elation,
Fear of extinction,
Fear of contemplation...

Numb minds and sleeping souls,
Destroying that which gives them life.
Turning glazed eyes from any form of truth,
They swim in chaos like salmon in the stream of life.

Small sparks of light flicker in the muck,
Seeming misplaced and otherworldly.

From afar...so afar...
A pattern of beauty is seen...
A pattern of swirling energy,
Free to grow and create
In the soil of its waste.

Epiphany

He heard her whisper softly in the night
As his head lay cradled on her breast.
He felt the steady rhythm of her heart
While he soared through dreams of green and blue.
His soul was filled with the wonder of her
As he felt the delicate balance of her body.
In his moment of greatest peace he felt her pain.
Waves of agony rolled through her ravaged flesh.
Sadness radiated from deep within her
Like that of a dying man whose life was left unfinished.
He felt the heavy burden on her spirit
As she bore the weight of her dying children.
He saw her burned and charred,
Suffocated and plundered,
No longer able to sustain or support...
And he cried out in agony for what he and his kind had done.

Waking in the first rays of the sun,
He saw a tiny flower
Emerging from the muddy pool of his tears.

www.ingramcontent.com/pod-product-compliance
Lightning Source LLC
Chambersburg PA
CBHW031956080426
42735CB00007B/416